CROCHET GARDEN

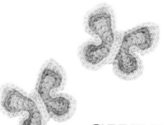

SUZANN THOMPSON

CROCHET GARDEN

Bunches of Flowers, Leaves, and Other Delights

LARK CRAFTS
Asheville

EDITOR
Valerie Van Arsdale Shrader

ASSISTANT EDITOR
Thom O'Hearn

ART DIRECTOR
Megan Kirby

ART ASSISTANT
Meagan Shirlen

PHOTOGRAPHER
Steve Mann

ILLUSTRATOR
Eva Reitzel

COVER DESIGNER
Megan Kirby

LARK CRAFTS

An Imprint of Sterling Publishing
387 Park Avenue South
New York, NY 10016

If you have questions or comments about
this book, please visit: larkcrafts.com

Library of Congress Cataloging-in-Publication Data

Thompson, Suzann.
  Crochet garden : bunches of flowers, leaves, and other delights / Suzann Thompson. -- 1st ed.
    p. cm.
  Includes bibliographical references and index.
  ISBN 978-1-60059-927-9 (alk. paper)
  1. Crocheting--Patterns. 2. Artificial flowers. I. Title.
  TT825.T486 2012
  746.43'4--dc23
                                            2011031991

10 9 8 7 6 5 4 3 2 1

First Edition

Published by Lark Crafts
An Imprint of Sterling Publishing Co., Inc.
387 Park Avenue South, New York, NY 10016

Text © 2012, Suzann Thompson

Photography © 2012, Lark Crafts, an Imprint of Sterling Publishing Co., Inc., unless otherwise specified

Illustrations © 2012, Lark Crafts, an Imprint of Sterling Publishing Co., Inc., unless otherwise specified

Distributed in Canada by Sterling Publishing,
c/o Canadian Manda Group, 165 Dufferin Street
Toronto, Ontario, Canada M6K 3H6

Distributed in the United Kingdom by GMC Distribution Services,
Castle Place, 166 High Street, Lewes, East Sussex, England BN7 1XU

Distributed in Australia by Capricorn Link (Australia) Pty Ltd.,
P.O. Box 704, Windsor, NSW 2756 Australia

Manufactured in China

ISBN 13: 978-1-60059-927-9

For information about custom editions, special sales, premium and corporate purchases, please contact Sterling Special Sales Department at 800-805-5489 or specialsales@sterlingpub.com.

For information about desk and examination copies available to college and university professors, requests must be submitted to academic@larkbooks.com. Our complete policy can be found at www.larkcrafts.com.

Contents

Introduction

My mother once told me about hunting wild mushrooms with her mother and brothers in the Frankenwald of Germany during World War II. She found more mushrooms than anyone else, because, as she says, "I had 'mushroom eyes.'"

While *Crochet Garden* was in progress, I had "flower eyes." I saw flowers everywhere! Hubcaps made me think of strange, futuristic flowers. The speaker at my bank's drive-through window looked like a Japanese mum.

Then we saw a movie about the Hubble Space Telescope in a 3D theater. The images were so beautiful they brought tears to my eyes. Of course, I could still see that many nebulae--or star nurseries as they were fondly referred to in the movie--look like flowers with bright, glowing centers. (See for yourself at the Hubble website.)

The word "flower" intrigued me, too. This book is about how to crochet the blooming parts of plants that we call flowers. However, people can flower too. If you cover something with blossoms, you flower it. Or when you come into the best, most productive, and rewarding stage of your career or your life, people say that you are flowering.

The fascinating connection between images and words figured in many of the designs in *Crochet Garden*. The designs are divided into four chapters:

- "Botanical Garden" has close to life-like interpretations of flowers and leaves.
- To bring you the designs in "Inspired Garden," I spent hours enthusiastically studying decorative art books, pretty chinaware, embroideries, and folk art.
- The designs in "International Garden" have a strong association with countries around the world (even if only in my own mind).
- In addition to some patterns for unusual flowers, "Fun and Fantastic Garden" is where you'll find the most word play. You may groan or you may laugh. I'll take it as a compliment either way.

What can you do with the flowers you crochet? Glue flowers to lampshades, refrigerator magnets, and scrapbook pages. Make pretty party invitations or unique personal stationery using your scanner and a color printer. I know readers of *Crochet Bouquet* used them for all sorts of things: from imprinting hand made pottery to adornments on hats for cancer patients.

Give children crocheted flowers, and watch their creative minds go to work. They tack them to bulletin boards, glue them to posters, and slip them under the vinyl covers of their ring-binders. My daughter Eva pinned flowers on a long, white dress and voilá! She was dressed as Persephone, goddess of spring, for a school assignment.

No matter what you use them for, I hope these patterns will fill your hours with pleasant crochet, and your home and workplace with colorful reminders of nature.

Let's gather our hooks and yarn, go forth, and flower!

Basics

yarn

You can use any type of yarn to crochet the flowers and other motifs in this book. If you use a bulky yarn, your flower will be big. A fine crochet thread will give you a cute little flower.

Most of the motifs in *Crochet Garden* use very little yarn, so you can use yarns left over from other projects.

Crochet Garden lists the exact yarns used for each flower and the resulting size of the flower. Use this information as you see fit but don't let it limit you in any way. Look for specific yarns in your local yarn shop. Shop owners are usually willing to special-order yarns that they don't have in stock. If your yarn shop is hours away, like mine, then the Internet is the next best place to buy yarn. Keep in mind that your computer screen may not show the precise color of each yarn.

With the exception of a few notable standbys, yarns and yarn colors tend to go in and out of fashion, just like hemlines and collar shapes. At some point in the future, many of the yarns and colors used in this book will be discontinued. Don't despair! Think of it as an excuse to try new yarns.

Compare the Sulfur Butterfly (page 31) made in bulky Lion Chenille (size 7.00mm/L-11 U.S. hook) to the very same pattern crocheted with Louet Euroflax Sport (3.50mm/E-4 U.S. hook). The larger butterfly was embellished with DMC Color Infusions Memory Thread.

WORKING WITH UNUSUAL YARNS

Before you make a big, fancy flower with an unusual yarn, take the time to figure out what the yarn is like. Make a small practice piece and note how the yarn behaves as you crochet. Weave in the ends and block the piece. Do the knots hold? Do the yarn ends stay woven in? How did the yarn take to blocking? Are you satisfied that the yarn will work for you? If your answer is 'yes', go ahead and make that big, fancy flower!

With a slick, slippery yarn such as DMC Satin embroidery floss (see the Violet, page 38), use a fray-stopping adhesive to keep knots and cut ends from slipping out. Block the flower thoroughly with steam, using a press cloth to protect the crochet.

Remember to crochet eyelash yarns from the wrong side, so the backside of the stitch shows at the front. The eyelashes tend to stay at the back of the stitch (see the Tabby Oval shown on this page).

When crocheting with vinyl yarn, lubricate your hook every minute or so with lotion or hand balm. To block a flower made from vinyl yarn, hand stretch it and hold for 30 seconds. * Turn the flower, stretch it from another angle, and hold for 30 seconds. Repeat from * until the flower stays the way you want it. Then stretch it, pin it to your blocking surface, and let it rest for several hours. If the motif is flat, hand stretch it, pin it, and place a book on top of it overnight.

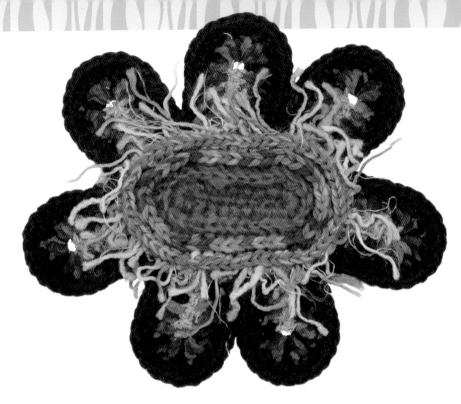

This Tabby Oval (page 64) is made from all kinds of yarns. My friends and family said, "It's so you, Suzann!" To show off the shaggy yarn (Crystal Palace Yarns Squiggle), I crocheted Rnd 5 from the wrong side. This meant I had to change the BPsc-sts of Rnd 5 to FPsc-sts, but it was worth the trouble.

stuffing

You'll need stuffing for a few of the three-dimensional motifs in *Crochet Garden*. I used polyester fiberfill, which is available at craft and quilting stores.

hooks and other hardware

To make the motifs in this book, you need these tools and supplies:

- Crochet hooks in various sizes
- Split-ring stitch markers
- Tapestry needle
- Scissors

To block the motifs, you need:

- A surface for pinning and ironing motifs, like an ironing board or a folded towel
- Pins
- A press cloth, such as a a clean tea towel or clean cloth diaper
- Iron

The projects in *Crochet Garden* will give you ideas for using the flowers. The projects may require additional supplies, which will be listed with the instructions.

Here are a few other things you might like to have on hand for embellishing flowers or for simple flower appliqué:

- Buttons
- Beads
- Fabric glue
- Sewing thread
- Sewing needles
- Safety pins

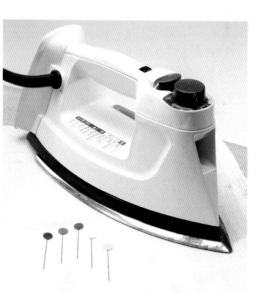

You can buy split-ring stitch markers or use paper clips or safety pins. If you're in a pinch, tie a short piece of yarn into a loop and use it for a stitch marker. You can untie the yarn or cut it away when you're finished. This sample is crocheted with Prism Yarns Tulle.

techniques

WHERE TO FIND BASIC CROCHET INSTRUCTIONS

To make room for more flower patterns, we decided to leave beginning crochet instructions out of *Crochet Garden*. If you don't know how to crochet, many excellent books, websites, and teachers are ready and waiting to guide you. Yarn or craft shops should be able to help you find beginning crochet classes or freelance teachers. Crochet guild members are usually eager to help beginners. For self-teaching, start at the Craft Yarn Council's website: www.craftyarncouncil.com. Follow the links to the crochet instruction pages and beyond.

Sometimes you need to see someone else doing a stitch so you can understand how it's done. Thank goodness for YouTube! A group of dedicated crochet experts has taken the time to create video tutorials of crochet stitches. Find them at www.youtube.com. Search "Crochet Stitches."

Just so you know that it can be done, let me share the story of a lady who attended a book signing I did for my previous book, *Crochet Bouquet*. It was a bright autumn day at Front Street Books in Alpine, Texas. The lady sat with *Crochet Bouquet* open in her lap, and a how-to-crochet book peeking out from underneath it. She consulted the how-to book frequently. That afternoon, she crocheted a daffodil—her first crochet project ever. The only stitch her how-to book didn't have was the htr, which is explained in this chapter.

STANDARDS & GUIDELINES FOR CROCHET AND KNITTING
Standard Yarn Weight System

Yarn Weight Symbol & Category Names	1 Super Fine	2 Fine	3 Light	4 Medium	5 Bulky	6 Super Bulky
Type of Yarns in Category	Sock, Fingering, Baby	Sport, Baby	DK, Light Worsted	Worsted, Afghan, Aran	Chunky, Craft, Rug	Bulky, Roving
Crochet Gauge* Ranges in Single Crochet to 4 inch	21-32 sts	16-20 sts	12-17 sts	11-14 sts	8-11 sts	5-9 sts
Recommended Hook in Metric Size Range	2.25-3.5 mm	3.5-4.5 mm	4.5-5.5 mm	5.5-6.5 mm	6.5-9 mm	9 mm and larger
Recommended Hook U.S. Size Range	B-1 to E-4	E-4 to 7	7 to I-9	I-9 to K-10½	K-10½ to M-13	M-13 and larger

Source: Craft Yarn Council of America's www.YarnStandards.com

Gauge circles are quicker than traditional gauge swatches, and they're useful, too! To measure your Gauge Circle, put it on top of the measuring tape.

gauge

Gauge refers to the tightness or looseness of your crochet stitches. Loose stitches make a project bigger and give it a softer hand. The same project crocheted tightly will be smaller and stiffer.

The motifs in *Crochet Garden* require a firm gauge, which is almost—but not quite—tight. The firm tension helps the motifs hold their shape. A firm gauge is neat and trim. It isn't floppy.

You'll know your tension is too tight if you have trouble inserting the hook into the stitches. If your tension is too loose, the flowers will lose some of their definition and may not be able to hold up their own weight.

The Craft Yarn Council's Standard Yarn Weight System chart (see chart on page 10), lists a range of hooks that work best with different yarns. For a firm gauge, try the smallest hook in the range.

Gauge is ingrained in our crochet culture, so every single motif in this book comes with a gauge measurement—but with a twist. By the time you crochet the traditional 4 x 4"/10 x 10cm gauge swatch, you probably could have completed at least one flower, and you'd know how it looked, and whether you'd do better with a larger or smaller hook. So instead of the traditional gauge swatch, we'll be making little Gauge Circles.

GAUGE CIRCLE

Ch 4, join with sl st in first ch to form a ring.

Rnd 1: Ch 2, 11 hdc in ring, cut thread, needle-join to first st of rnd.

To measure the Gauge Circle, place it on top of a measuring tape or ruler. Arrange it so the inch or centimeter mark barely shows at one edge of it. Note which mark shows at the opposite edge of the piece, remove the gauge

circle, and determine how wide it is (its diameter). If your gauge circle is larger than mine, you might want to use a smaller hook; if your circle is smaller, try a larger hook.

Good things about the Gauge Circle: You'll have lots of practice with needle-joining. You can use Gauge Circles as flower centers and fillers in flower cloth (page 16).

HTR: ITS HISTORY AND HOW-TO

Crochet lends itself to gentle curves, beginning with the shortest slip stitch and moving through sc, hdc, dc, and then—oh my!—there's a big jump between the height of the dc and the tall tr stitches.

The tr may buckle or bulge when it's placed next to a dc because of the difference in the height of the stitches. This bothered me a lot when I was a young crocheter. "If the half-double is the step between a sc and a dc," I reasoned, "then the step between a dc and a trc must be a half-treble!"

Half-treble or htr is indeed the missing step. It's taller than a dc but shorter than a tr. The htr works on the same principle as the hdc, only it begins with one extra yo. Here's how to make an htr:

> Yo twice. Insert hook in next stitch and draw up a loop (4 loops on hook).
>
> Yo and draw through two loops (3 loops on hook).
>
> Yo and draw through remaining loops (1 loop on hook).

FRONT LOOP, BACK LOOP— WHAT'S THE DIFFERENCE?

Unless instructed otherwise, we catch the top two loops of any crochet stitch as we work. Sometimes a pattern directs you to crochet in the front or back loop only. The front loop is the one that is closest to you as you work, regardless of whether you're working in the round or back and forth. The back loop is the one that is away from you as you work.

Why do patterns sometimes specify that you crochet into the front or back loop only?

1. When you crochet into the back loop only, the unused front loop gives definition to the row or round below. It makes a subtle outline, as you can see after Rnd 3 of the Samarkand Sunflower (at right).

2. When you crochet a row into the front loop only, and then another row into the back loop only of the same row, you create two rows where before you had only one. This is a useful tool for crochet construction. The Flamenco Flower (page 94) uses this technique, as well as the Pinecone pictured here.

3. Working rows back and forth into the back loop creates a corrugated fabric, lending texture to a design. The Any-Color-Pinks, shown here, take advantage of this technique.

4. Working a round into the front loop only bends the round toward you. On the other hand, crocheting a round into the back loop bends the round away from you. This is another useful construction technique.

Inside the petal round of this small Samarkand Sunflower, look for the outline just inside Rnd 3. It's made by the unused front loops of Rnd 2 (red). This sample is made with Universal Yarns Fibra Natura Flax.

Crocheting into the back loop only as you make the cone part of the Pinecone (page 118) creates a line of front loops that spirals around the cone. Here, I'm about one-third of the way through Rnd 10, where I'm crocheting into those front loops to form the scales of the pinecone made from Universal Yarns Fibra Natura Exquisite Bamboo.

The corrugated blooms of Any-Color-Pinks are made by crocheting into the back loop of each row. This sample is Prism Yarns Symphony.

decreasing

To decrease in crochet, you begin 2 (or more) sts but stop short of the last yo and pull through. Only when you have begun all the sts you want to decrease do you yo and pull through all their unfinished loops. On the next row or rnd, you will see one stitch where there were 2 (or more).

A more specific example is "dc2tog," which means "double crochet 2 sts together." Here's how:

> Yo, insert into next st, yo, and pull up a loop (3 loops on hook).
>
> Yo, pull through 2 loops (2 loops on hook). Now the dc is begun but stopped just short of the final yo/ pull-through.
>
> Yo, insert into next st, yo, and pull up a loop (4 loops on hook).
>
> Yo, pull through 2 loops (3 loops on hook). The 2nd dc is begun and stopped just short of its final yo/ pull-through.
>
> To finish the dc2tog, yo, and pull through all lps on hook.

Some patterns require you to decrease two stitches of different sizes, like "dc-hdc-dec." This means "decrease by crocheting a dc and a hdc together." It operates on the same basic principle:

> Yo, insert into next st, yo, and pull up a loop (3 loops on hook).

A Gambel Oak Leaf (page 21) has two dc-hdc-decreases. Here, the dc-hdc-dec on Row 5 is in progress, awaiting the final yo and pull-through all loops on hook. I used Dale of Norway Falk for the sample.

Yo, pull through 2 loops (2 loops on hook). Now the dc is begun but stopped just short of the final yo/pull-through.

Yo, insert into next st, yo, pull up a loop. (5 loops on hook) The hdc is begun but stopped before the last yo/pull-through.

To finish the dc-hdc-tog, yo, and pull through all lps on hook.

WORKING IN THE FREE LOOPS OF THE CHAIN

When you work a row of stitches into the chain, then rotate the work and crochet into the chain again, we call it "working into the free loops of the chain." It's a good technique for shaping crochet.

In this photo, Rnd 3 of the Iris (page 28) is in progress. The first petal is done. The first 3 sc of the second petal are worked in the free loops of the chain of Rnd 2.

needle-join

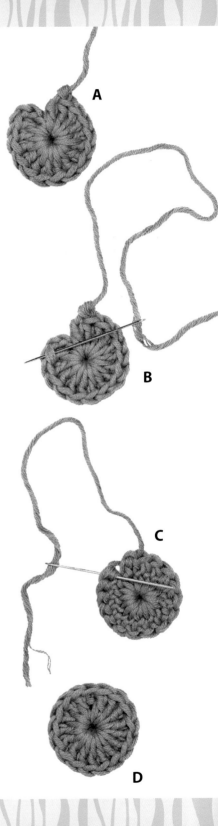

For a seamless-looking finish, join rounds of crochet with the needle-join.

Complete the last st of the round.

With the hook still in the last loop, cut the yarn, leaving an end about 4"/10 cm long.

Pull the hook straight up from the stitch, so the yarn end will come out of the top of the stitch. (Photo A shows the yarn end pulled through.)

Thread the yarn into a tapestry needle.

Look at the top of the first stitch of the round. This may be a ch-3 (acting as the 1st dc, as in the sample here) or ch-2 (acting as the 1st hdc)—either way, the last ch is the top of the stitch.

Following the yarn loop at the top of the 1st st, insert your needle from front to back, under the loops of the 2nd st. (Photo B)

A

B

C

D

Insert the needle into the top of the last stitch, catching the back loop and the yarn loop under that. (Photo C shows the sample from the back.)

The yarn comes out at the back of the work. Tighten the new loop to match the loops at the top of the other stitches.

The original top of the 1st st may add extra bulk at this join. Push or pull it to the back, and weave the yarn end through it to keep it at the back.

The finished join doesn't look like a join at all (Photo D).

By replacing the top loop of the 1st st with a needle-join, you'll preserve the correct number of stitches in the round. This is important for flowers like the Samarkand Sunflower (page 60), where you'll be crocheting another round into the one you just finished.

A needle-join can be for looks only, like when you join the stem of a leaf to its base. You can also join with a sl-st, but this makes an unsightly bump. A needle-join is well worth the time for a better finish.

blocking

I know, I know—many crocheters never block anything! This is fine for certain yarns and projects, but your crocheted flowers and leaves will behave better (none of that pesky curling) and have a professional-looking finish if you block them.

Wool, mohair, linen, and cotton respond well to steam blocking. Blends of these natural fibers with synthetics do fine with steam blocking as well. I'm more comfortable using the cool, wet-blocking method with silk, silk blends, and synthetic fibers. If you have doubts about how your yarn will respond, block a small sample as an experiment.

COOL, WET BLOCKING

Douse the motif with water. Squeeze out as much water as you can. You can roll the motif in a towel and press out more of the moisture, but DO NOT WRING IT. Spread the motif on your blocking surface. Unfurl it and stretch out the points, petals, and leaves. For best results, pin the points of the leaves and petals, especially if they curl stubbornly. Let dry.

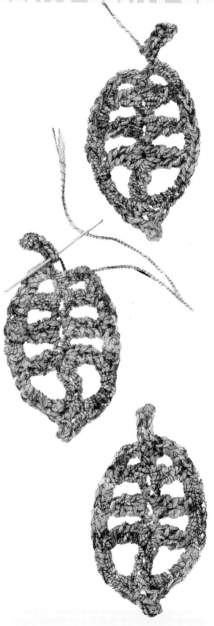

Needle-join the Cut-Out Leaf's (page 82) stem to a loop at the base of the leaf. Since you're not concerned here, at the finish, with a particular stitch count, join the stem wherever it will look best. This leaf is made with Berroco Origami.

STEAM BLOCKING

Heat the iron (you can use steam or not). Wet a press cloth and wring out the excess water.

Spread the motif on your blocking surface. Unfurl it and stretch out the points, petals, and leaves. Pin the points of the leaves and petals for best results. Lay the press cloth over the motif and hold a hot iron over it lightly. The steam will go into the motif. Then remove the press cloth and make sure the motif looks the way you want it to. Let cool and dry.

The three-dimensional flowers in the book can be blocked if necessary. Wrap the motif in the wet press cloth, then use the iron to gently roll the motif back and forth. Hold the iron lightly over the motif. You can also choose specific parts to block, such as the sepals of the Mexican Hat (page 24).

flower cloth

Flower cloth is made from crocheted flowers and other motifs, which are sewn together in any shape. The Flower Cloth Scarf on page 129 is an example of flower cloth.

First, decide what you want to make. It can be anything you can cut from fabric. To familiarize yourself with the technique, begin with a flat project, like a scarf, table runner, or doily. Cut the shape of your project from a piece of sturdy fabric. The fabric won't be part of the finished project. Gather yarns of various sizes, textures,

and fiber content. I usually try to unify my yarn choices by picking yarns in one color family, or sticking to a few colors. You can also stick to one type of yarn. Anything goes!

Crochet enough motifs to cover your fabric, plus a few extras. Make some small motifs, like Gauge Circles (page 11), or motifs in lightweight yarns. Weave in all the ends and block the motifs. Arrange the motifs

Here's a Paired Leaflet Frond (page 127) prepared for blocking. After unfurling and stretching the leaves, I pinned their points. Once this frond has been blocked and cooled, the leaves will stay nice and flat (as they are here) after the pins are removed. Compare with the unblocked frond. Samples are made with Cascade Yarns Cascade 220.

facedown on the fabric, with their edges touching wherever possible. Whenever you have a gap that is too large for your liking but too small for a regular motif, use a Gauge Circle or tiny motif to fill it in. Safety-pin the motifs in place.

Use sewing thread to sew the edges of the motifs together. Since the motifs are facedown, the sewing stitches will be on the wrong side of the work. Keep the stitches small. You'll need to tack and cut thread fairly often. Remove the pins and fabric. Admire your finished work!

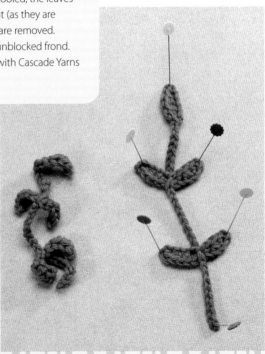

The Flower Cloth Scarf, a flower cloth project, is in progress here. The motifs are safety-pinned to a piece of fabric. See the finished project on page 129.

contact me

If you need help with any pattern in this book, please contact me. At my book blog, "Curious and Crafty Readers," I'll be hosting more-or-less monthly crochet-a-longs with patterns from this book for at least two years after it's published. At my blog, you'll also find tutorials (feel free to ask for them), ideas for using crocheted flowers, and more. Please leave a comment at the blog, or contact me by email. Find a link to my email address at the blog site, www.textilefusion.com/bookblog.

Ravelry (www.ravelry.com) is a free, online knitting and crochet community, where my tag is "textilefusion." We have a flower crochet-a-long group on Ravelry, too. Look for flower crochet-a-longs at Crochetville (www.crochetville.org), at the Crochet Bouquet/Crochet Garden page on Facebook (www.facebook.com), and at Yahoo groups (www.groups.yahoo.com). Please send me your comments and suggestions, too. I'd love to hear from you!

tips

PATTERN READING

- To help you orient yourself in a row or round, some instructions specify where to place each stitch, like this: "sc in each of next 2 chs, (sc, ch 1, hdc) in next ch, (dc, htr) in next st …"

- When the stitch placement is not specified, place each new stitch in the next stitch of the row below, unless otherwise instructed. For instance, if the instructions read, "2 sl sts, sc, hdc, (2 dc) in next st, 4 hdc," then you should "sl st into each of the next 2 sts, sc in the next st, hdc in the next stitch, work 2 dc into the next st, hdc in each of the next 4 sts."

- Parentheses ( ) and brackets [ ] are intended to group stitches. For instance, "(2 sc) in the next st," alerts you to the fact that the 2 sc-sts are together and you need to read further to find out how they will be used. In this case, you will place them both in the next stitch.

- Parentheses and brackets also group stitches for repetition: (dc2tog, dc 3) 4 times = dc2tog, dc 3, dc2tog, dc 3, dc2tog, dc 3, dc2tog, dc 3.

- Single asterisks *, double asterisks **, and double crosses ‡, are markers in the pattern. Ignore them until the instructions refer to them. Most of the time, you'll see instructions something like "Repeat from * 3 times." You have already followed the instructions once. Now repeat them 3 times. When you're finished, you will have followed the instructions 4 times in all.

- When instructions seem overwhelming, try making a flip book (see page 18), or ask someone to read the instructions aloud to you. Reading a pattern aloud takes some skill, because the reader has to know how to pace the reading, and how much to read so the crocheter can make sense of it all. You'll both need some patience to make this work.

- *Crochet Garden* was written using abbreviations of US crochet terms. This chart gives the UK equivalents:

U.S. ABBR	U.K. ABBR
sc	dc
Hdc	Htr
Dc	Tr
Htr	Hdtr
Trc	Dtr
BPsc	BPdc
BPdc	BPtr
Dc-CL	Tr-CL
Tr-CL	Dtr-CL

FLIP BOOKS FOR EASIER PATTERN READING

Let's borrow a trick that knitters use when column after column of instructions overwhelm them (lace patterns are often the worst). Knitters frequently copy patterns onto index cards, one row per card. Then they punch the corner of each card and fasten the bunch together with a binding ring or a loop of yarn.

You can do this with the instructions in *Crochet Garden*, too. As you copy the pattern, break up each row into manageable chunks. For instance, write instructions in parentheses on separate lines. You'll be amazed at how much better you understand a pattern after you write it out. As you crochet, look only at the card that has instructions for the row or round you're working on. As soon as you're done with that row, go to the next card.

BEYOND BEGINNER

"Are these patterns easy?" That's the question some of you are undoubtedly asking about the projects in *Crochet Garden*. Sure, some of them are easy. And some seem easy to me but require my close attention. You've probably tried patterns that were difficult at first, but when you figured out how they worked, they became easy for you.

In my experience, crocheters tend to underestimate their level of skill. People who have crocheted for years still claim to be beginners. How can a person move beyond beginning crochet and feel confident enough to tackle any crochet pattern? If you're ready to develop your crochet skills, the first step is to *practice with purpose* by paying attention as you crochet.

- Notice how the loops form stitches.
- Examine the stitches from front and back.
- Learn to identify the stitches that form a pattern.
- Watch how certain stitch combinations alter the shape of the work.
- Challenge yourself by trying intermediate and advanced patterns, knowing that you can find help if you need it (see "Contact Me," page 17).

To further develop your skills, consider participating in the Crochet Guild of America (CGOA) Master of Advanced Stitches and Techniques program. The program guides you in learning new stitches and techniques. It will make you a better crocheter. Find more information at www.crochet.org. The CGOA hosts annual crochet conferences, with workshops for crocheters of all skill levels. If you've never experienced a crochet conference, you should try it!

DOING WHAT IT TAKES

This is for the impetuous crocheters—those who feel their projects should be finished the moment they put down their hooks. "Phooey on all that silly blocking and sewing!" they say. I used to say that, too, but now I know better. So take my advice: If you want your crochet projects to be the best they can be, you must do what it takes.

This sounds ridiculously obvious, but it took me many years of crocheting and crafting to understand and accept what it means to, "Do what it takes."

What does it take to do any crochet project? You have to decipher the pattern, learn the techniques you need, gather supplies, crochet, and do the finishing work.

What does it take to make a Tabby Oval? You have to learn how to needle-join the rounds.

I like to make projects with lots of colors, so I must weave in many yarn ends. That's what it takes when a crocheter use lots of colors.

Do you like that Byzantine Beauty? You're going to have to crochet it in sections, and then sew the pieces together. That's what it takes.

Are you going to glue a crocheted flower to your shoe? Then you need to wait for the glue to set before you wear the shoes to a guild meeting. That's what it takes.

You'll see what I mean.

Embrace the idea that crochet is only one part of a larger project. With this change in perspective, you'll be more motivated to sew pieces together, block flowers, and wait for glue to dry. It takes a few extra minutes. But the time you spend now, doing what it takes, will reward you with feelings of satisfaction and accomplishment whenever you see the beautiful work you made with your own hands.

Botanical Garden

Begonia

The simple shape of begonia flowers allows their glistening, translucent color to shine. When you sew this flower onto a project, let the small petals bend forward at the edges, as they will do naturally.

SKILL LEVEL
Beginner

MATERIALS & TOOLS
2 colors of yarn of similar weight: petal color (A), stamen color (B)

Hook: Appropriate size hook to achieve a firm gauge with selected yarn

Tapestry needle

SPECIAL ABBREVIATION
Htr (half treble crochet): Yo 2 times, insert hook in stitch and draw up a loop (4 loops on hook), yo and draw through 2 loops (3 loops on hook), yo and draw through 3 loops (1 loop left on hook).

FOR THESE FLOWERS WE USED

Cascade Pima Tencel (50% Peruvian cotton, 50% tencel; 1.75oz/50g = 109yd/99m): (A) color salmon #9504; (B) color yellow #258—light weight yarn; (3)

GAUGE CIRCLE
(see page 11) = 15⁄16"/2.4cm worked on 4.00mm (size G-6 U.S.) hook

FINISHED MATERIALS
2⅝"/8.7cm x 2⅜"/6cm

Spud and Chloë Sweater (55% superwash wool, 45% organic cotton; 3.5oz/100g = 160yd/146m): (A) color Jelly Bean #7513 or color Watermelon #7512; (B) color Firefly #7505—medium weight yarn; (4)

GAUGE CIRCLE
(see page 11) = 1¼"/3cm worked on 5.00mm (size H-8 U.S.) hook

FINISHED MATERIALS
3.5"/8.8cm x 3"/7.6cm

INSTRUCTIONS

Flower
With A, ch 4, join with sl st in first ch to form a ring.

Rnd 1: *Ch 3, 4 dc in ring, ch 3, sl st in ring, ch 5, sl st in 3rd ch from hook, ch 2, sl st in ring; rep from * once.

Rnd 2: *Sc in each of next 2 chs, (sc, ch 1, hdc) in next ch, (dc, htr) in next st, 2 tr, (htr, dc) in next st, (hdc, ch 1, sc) in next ch, sc in each of next 2 ch. Sc in ring, 2 sc in next ch-2 sp, working around the top of petal (3 hdc, ch 2, sl st in 2nd ch from hook, 3 hdc) in ch-3 sp, working down the other side of the petal, 2 sc in next ch-2 sp, sc in ring; rep from * once. Needle-join to first st of rnd.

Stamens
With B, *ch 4, sl st in 3rd ch from hook and rem ch; rep from * 2 or 3 times. Fasten off. Use tail to tack first stamen to last stamen. Take both yarn ends through the center of the flower and stitch the base of each stamen in place.

Finishing
Weave in ends. Block very gently, allowing the smaller side petals to fold upward.

Gambel Oak Leaves

The Gambel Oak is native to the state of Colorado. These leaves remind me of a beautiful June day, when our family hiked around Mesa Verde National Park.

SKILL LEVEL
Intermediate

MATERIALS & TOOLS
1 leaf-colored yarn (A)

Hook: Appropriate size hook to achieve a firm gauge with selected yarn

Tapestry needle

SPECIAL ABBREVIATIONS
Dc-hdc-tog: Yo, insert hook in next stitch, yo and draw up a loop, yo and draw through 2 loops on hook, yo, insert hook in next st, yo and draw up a loop (4 loops on hook), yo and draw through remaining loops on hook.

Hdc2tog: Half double crochet 2 stitches together

FOR THESE LEAVES WE USED
Prism Indulgence (68% silk, 15% wool, 12% kid mohair, 5% nylon; 2oz/56g = 92yd/84m): (A) color Copper Penny and Mojave—medium weight yarn; **(4)**

GAUGE CIRCLE
(see page 11) = 1 1/8"/2.9cm worked on 5.00mm (size H-8 U.S.) hook

FINISHED MATERIALS
3⁹⁄₁₆"/9.1cm x 3⅞"/9.8cm (small leaf with bent stem); 3⁷⁄₁₆"/8.7cm x 4¾"/12.1cm (big leaf with bent stem)

Berroco Ultra® Alpaca (50% super fine alpaca, 50% Peruvian wool; 3.5oz/100g = 215yd/198m): (A) color light brown #6202—light weight yarn; **(3)**

GAUGE CIRCLE
(see page 11) = 1"/2.5cm worked on 4.00mm (size G-6 U.S.) hook

FINISHED MATERIALS
3"/7.6cm x 3¼"/8.2cm (small leaf with bent stem)

Cascade Luna (100% Peruvian cotton; 1.75oz/50g = 82yd/75m): (A) color green #755—bulky weight yarn; **(5)**

GAUGE CIRCLE
(see page 11) = 1⁵⁄₁₆"/3.3cm worked on 6.00mm (size J-10 U.S.) hook

FINISHED MATERIALS
3⅞"/9.8cm x 5"/12.2cm (big leaf with bent stem)

INSTRUCTIONS

Large Leaf (see page 22)

Row 1(RS): Ch 6, hdc in 3rd ch from hook, hdc, dc2tog, ch 2, turn.

Row 2: Sk the turning ch, hdc2tog in first 2 sts. Some sts rem unworked. Ch 9, turn.

Row 3: Dc in 4th ch from hook, 4 dc, dc-hdc-tog, ignore turning ch from previous row, ch 2, turn.

Row 4: Sk the turning ch, hdc2tog in first 2 sts, hdc. Some sts rem unworked. Ch 8, turn.

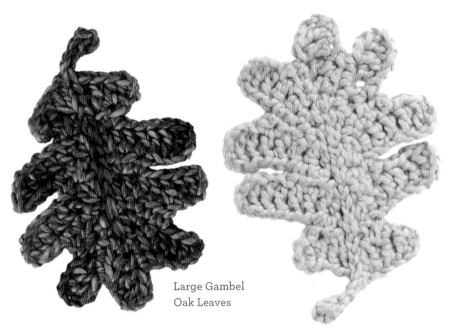

Large Gambel
Oak Leaves

Row 5: Dc in 4th ch from hook, 4 dc, dc-hdc-tog, ignore turning ch from previous row, ch 1, turn.

Row 6: Sc2tog, hdc, dc. Some sts rem unworked. Ch 6, turn.

Row 7: Dc in 4th ch from hook, 2 dc, hdc, sc2tog, ch 1, turn.

Row 8: Sc, 2 hdc. Some sts rem unworked. Ch 5, turn. You have worked one half of the leaf, from its middle to one side.

Row 9: Dc in 4th ch from hook, 2 dc, hdc, sc, ch 1, turn. You just made the top lobe of the leaf. From now on, you'll work the other half of the leaf, joining it to the first half, down the middle, as noted.

Row 10: Sc, 2 hdc. Some sts rem unworked. Ch 5, turn.

Row 11: Dc in 4th ch from hook, 2 dc, hdc, (2 sc) in next st, join with sl st to the base of row 7, ch 1, turn. A gap forms when you join the lobes, and that's fine. We'll fill those in later.

Row 12: Sk the sl st, (2 sc) in first sc, hdc, dc. Some sts rem unworked. Ch 5, turn.

Row 13: Dc in 4th ch from hook, 4 dc, (dc, hdc) in next st, join with sl st at the base of row 5, ch 1, turn.

Row 14: Sk the sl st, (2 hdc) in first hdc, hdc. Some sts rem unworked. Ch 6, turn.

Row 15: Dc in 4th ch from hook, 4 dc, (dc, hdc) in next st, join with sl st at the base of row 3, ch 1, turn.

Row 16: Sk the sl st, (2 hdc) in first hdc. Some sts rem unworked. Ch 3, turn.

Row 17: Hdc in 3rd ch from hook, hdc, (2 dc) in next st, join with sl st at the base of row 1.

STEM

Ch 6, hdc in 3rd ch from hook, sl st in rem ch.

CENTRAL VEIN

Stretch the leaf from side to side to see the spaces you created when you joined the lobes to each other. Now that you know where they are, look at the RS of the leaf and hold the yarn underneath the leaf (or at the WS of the leaf). Insert hook in the first sp in the center of the leaf, ch 2 or 3 (you are making the ch as your hook goes "through" the leaf). With the yarn still at the WS of the leaf, sl st in the st that joins the lobes. Continue filling the spaces with ch and sl st in the sts where the lobes join tog. End with a sl st just past the last sp. Fasten off. Use hook to take the yarn end through the leaf back to the WS of the leaf.

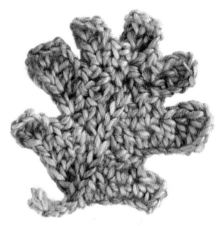

Small Gambel
Oak Leaves

Small Leaf

Row 1 (RS): Ch 9, dc in 4th ch from hook, 3 hdc, dc2tog, ch 3, turn.

Row 2: Sk turning ch from last row, dc2tog in the first 2 sts, hdc. Some sts rem unworked. Ch 9, turn.

Row 3: Tr in 5th ch from hook, 2 htr, dc, hdc, dc2tog, ch 3, turn. Ignore turning ch of last row.

Row 4: Sk turning ch from last row, dc2tog in the first 2 sts, hdc. Some sts rem unworked. Ch 6, turn.

Row 5: Dc in 4th ch from hook, dc, hdc, sc2tog, ch 1, turn. Ignore turning ch of last row.

Row 6: Sc, hdc. Some sts rem unworked. Ch 5, turn. You have worked one half of the leaf, from its middle to one side.

Row 7: Dc in 4th ch from hook, dc, hdc, sl st, ch 1, turn. You just made the top lobe of the leaf. From now on, you'll work the other half of the leaf, joining it to the first half, down the middle, as noted.

Row 8: Sc, hdc. Some sts rem unworked. Ch 5, turn.

Row 9: Dc in 4th ch from hook, dc, hdc, (2 sc) in next st, join with sl st to the base of row 5, ch 1, sl st in base of row 4.

Row 10: Sk the sl sts, (2 dc) in first sc, hdc. Some sts rem unworked. Ch 7, turn.

Row 11: Tr in 5th ch from hook, 2 htr, dc, hdc, (2 dc) in next st, join with sl st to the base of row 3, ch 1, sl st in base of row 2.

Row 12: Sk the sl sts, (2 dc) in first dc, hdc. Some sts rem unworked. Ch 5, turn.

Row 13: Dc in 4th ch from hook, 3 hdc, (2 dc) in next st, join with sl st to the base of row 1.

STEM

Ch 6, hdc in 3rd ch from hook, sl st in rem ch.

CENTRAL VEIN

Work as for Central Vein in Large Leaf.

Finishing

Weave in ends. Block gently. Stretch the turning ch at the end of each lobe from side to side, to flatten the tips of the lobes.

Mexican Hat

This showy summer wildflower blankets the roadsides of Texas and even some front yards, like mine! Sew it sideways onto a pin finding for a beautiful brooch.

Double Flower
Mexican Hat

SKILL LEVEL
Intermediate

MATERIALS & TOOLS
4 colors of yarn of similar weight: cone color (A), two petal colors (B and C), greenery color (D)

Hook: Appropriate size hook to achieve a firm gauge with selected yarn

Stuffing

Tapestry needle

SPECIAL ABBREVIATION
Htr (half treble crochet): Yo 2 times, insert hook in stitch and draw up a loop (4 loops on hook), yo and draw through 2 loops (3 loops on hook), yo and draw through 3 loops (1 loop left on hook).

PATTERN NOTE
On rnd 12 of the Single Flower and Double Flower, sl st in the back loop of the sc at the base of each petal. However, you will be looking at the underside of the flower, so back loops will seem like front loops. Because you are working in the round, in the established direction, I will refer to the loops as if you were working on the right side of the work.

INSTRUCTIONS

Single Flower

With A, ch 4, join with sl st in first ch to form a ring.

Rnd 1: 6 sc in ring.

Rnd 2: (2 sc) in first sc of rnd 1, 2 sc, (2 sc) in next sc, 2 sc—8 sc.

Rnds 3-7: Sc in each st around.

Rnd 8: *Ch 3, sk 1 st, sc in next st; rep from * 3 times. Stuff the cone lightly, using the end of your hook to push the stuffing in.

Rnd 9: *Folding the next ch-3 sp toward the outside of the cone so it is out of the way, sc in the skipped st in rnd 8; rep from * 3 times. Join with sl st to first sc of rnd. Fasten off. Weave in ends—4 sc.

Rnd 10: Join B with sl st in a ch-3 sp from rnd 8, *(ch 2 for the side of the petal, dc, htr, dc, ch 2 for the other side of the petal, sl st) in same sp. Ch 2 between petals, sl st in next ch-3 sp; rep from * twice. Ch 2, (dc, htr, dc, ch 2, sl st) in same sp. Ch 2, sl st in first st of rnd. For the single flower, fasten off, cut yarn and weave in end. For the double flower, fasten off but do not cut yarn—4 petals with ch 2 between petals.

FOR THESE FLOWERS WE USED

Berroco Ultra® Alpaca (50% super fine alpaca, 50% Peruvian wool; 3.5oz/100g = 215yd/198m): (A) color purple #62171; (B) color orange #6263 or red #6236; (C) color yellow #6225; (D) color green #6273—light weight yarn; (3)

GAUGE CIRCLE
(see page 11) = 1"/2.5cm worked on 4.00mm (size G-6 U.S.) hook

FINISHED MATERIALS
2¾"/7cm x 3½"/9cm (single); 2¾"/7cm x 4¼"/11cm (double)

Caron International Naturally Caron Country (25% merino wool, 75% microdenier acrylic; 3oz/85g = 185yd/170m): (A) color Spice House #0018; (B) color Gilded Age #0011; (C) color Loden Forest #0020—medium weight yarn; (4)

GAUGE CIRCLE
(see page 11) = 1"/2.5cm worked on 4.00mm (size G-6 U.S.) hook

FINISHED MATERIALS
3"/7.5cm x 4½"/11.5cm (double flower)

Single Flower
Mexican Hat

Rnd 11: Join C with *3 sc in ch-2 sp at the side of a petal. (2 hdc) in next dc, (2 dc) in htr, (2 hdc) in next dc, 3 sc in ch-2 sp on the other side of the petal. Sc in the sc between the ch-3 sp from rnd 8, catching the ch-2 sp from rnd 10 inside the stitch; rep from * 3 times. For the single flower, needle-join to first st of rnd and weave in ends. If you plan to make the double flower, sl st in BL of first sc of rnd.

Continuing with the single flower, make the sepals:

Rnd 12 (sepal rnd): See Pattern Note, above. Join D with sl st in BL of first sc at the base of any petal. *Looking at the bottom side of the flower, ch 1, sl st in BL of last sc of the petal, ch 7, sl st in 3rd ch from hook. Working along ch, 3 sc, hdc, then sl st in BL of first sc of the next petal; rep from * 3 times.

Rnd 13: Looking at the bottom side of the flower, and keeping the sepals toward the petals and out of the way, sc in each ch-1 sp of the previous rnd.

STEM

Ch 20, hdc in 3rd ch from hook, sc in each rem ch, sl st in 3rd sc of the previous rnd.

Double Flower

Work instructions for Single Flower through rnd 11, following special instructions for the Double Flower in rnds 10 and 11.

Rnd 12: See Pattern Note, above. Continuing in the same direction with C and *looking at the underside of the petal, ch 1, sl st in BL of last sc of the petal, ch 3, sl st in BL of first sc of the next petal; rep from * 2 times. Ch 1, sl st in last sc of the petal, ch 3, sl st in first st of the rnd.

Rnd 13: With B, *(sl st, ch 2, dc, htr, dc, ch 2, sl st) in next ch-3 sp, ch 2; rep from * 3 times. Join with sl st in ch-3 sp at beg of rnd. Fasten off, cut yarn, weave in ends.

Rnd 14: With C, *3 sc in ch-2 sp at the side of a petal. (2 hdc) in next dc, (3 dc) in htr, (2 hdc) in next dc, 3 sc in ch-2 sp. Tip the flower so you can see underneath the petals, sc in ch-1 sp from rnd 12 underneath the next completed petal, catching the B-colored ch-2 sp inside the st; rep from * 3 times. Cut yarn and needle join to first st of rnd. Weave in ends.

Rnds 15 and 16 and Stem: Work rnds 12 and 13 and Stem of Single Flower.

Finishing

Weave in ends. Wrap the sepals, 2 at a time, in a moist cloth and steam with the very edge of the iron. Unwrap and straighten them as much as possible. Leave the rest of the flower unblocked.

Bluebell

Blue blankets of wild hyacinth cover the woodland floor in the early spring near our former home in Sheffield, England. Make these pretty flowers in different shades of blue for a natural look.

SKILL LEVEL
Intermediate

MATERIALS & TOOLS
1 or 2 colors of yarn of similar weight: blue or desired flower color (A), green stem color (B)

Hook: Appropriate size hook to achieve a firm gauge with selected yarn

Tapestry needle

PATTERN NOTE
You can vary the pattern by making the body of the flower longer or shorter. If desired, change to green to make the stem or add beaded or crocheted stamens.

INSTRUCTIONS

Flower
Petal Row: With A, *ch 10, hdc in 3rd ch from hook, 7 hdc; rep from * 4 times. In each petal, the hdc in the 3rd ch from hook is the "first" hdc, and the final hdc is the "last" hdc. Do not turn. Continue as follows:

Curl Row (WS): Rotate your work until you see the sides of the 5 "last" hdc from the petal row, ch 1. *Insert hook under the next sideways hdc. Curl the petal to the back of the work, insert hook under the "first" hdc of the petal (this hdc will also be sideways, and the ch-2 sp will be underneath your hook). Yo, draw up a lp, yo and draw through the 2 lps on your hook to complete a sc. Sc in the next ch, which also has the "last" hdc in it; rep from * 4 times. Ch 1, turn.

Bell Rnd 1(RS): Sc in each sc across. Bring petals into a ring so that they curl to the outside of the flower. Sc in the first st of this row, joining it into a rnd.

Rnds 2-6: Sc in each sc around—10 sts.

Rnd 7: *Sk 1 st, sc in next st; rep from * 4 times—5 sts.

Stem
With B, ch 6, sc in 2nd ch from hook, sl st in each rem ch. Cut yarn and tack the end of the stem in the st across from its base.

Finishing
Weave in ends. The flower will hold its shape for many possible uses, but if you want to keep the flower from being squashed flat, push a small wad of stuffing into the bell. Friction will hold it in place; for extra safety, tack it as you weave in ends or with a few stitches of sewing thread in such a way that the stitches will disappear into the crochet fabric.

Dampen the curled petals. Roll each petal back and forth between finger and thumb, to make it as roundly curved as you can. Set flower down, stem up, and petals splayed out. Let dry.

FOR THESE FLOWERS WE USED
Cascade 220 Wool (100% Peruvian Highland wool; 3.5oz/100g = 220yd/200m): (A) color light blue #7815, violet #9467, royal blue #7818; (B) color green #4912 or #7814—medium weight yarn;

GAUGE CIRCLE
(see page 11) = 1"/2.5cm worked on 4.00mm (size G-6 U.S.) hook

FINISHED MATERIALS
2 1/16"/5.2cm x 2 1/8"/5.4cm (excluding stem)

Cascade Ultra Pima (100% Pima cotton; 3.5oz/100g = 220yd/200m): (A) color ice blue #3731; (B) color green #3739—sport weight yarn;

GAUGE CIRCLE
(see page 11) = 7/8"/2.2cm worked on 3.50mm (size E-4 U.S.) hook

FINISHED MATERIALS
1 5/8"/4.2cm x 1 3/4"/4.4cm

Iris

As a child, I pored over the full-page iris advertisements in my mother's old *Flower and Garden* magazines, choosing most of the irises on the page for my dream garden.

SKILL LEVEL
Intermediate

MATERIALS & TOOLS
3 or 4 colors of yarn of similar weight: yellow for pollen (A), two petal colors (B and C), greenery (D). Use a yarn with some body to it. Soft, floppy yarns won't work well

Hook: Appropriate size hook to achieve a firm gauge with selected yarn

Two split stitch markers or marker substitutes

Small amount of stuffing

Tapestry needle

PATTERN NOTE
In rounds 3 and 5, work up one side of a petal, in the 3 chains around its end, and down the other side. The chains are sometimes difficult to see, so save time by identifying the 3 chains at the end of the petal and counting back 7 stitches, which is where you will place your first petal stitch.

INSTRUCTIONS

Flower
With A, ch 4, join with sl st in first ch to form a ring.

Rnd 1 (RS): Ch 1, 6 sc in ring, join with sl st to first st of rnd.

Rnd 2: *Sl st in FL of next st, ch 10, dc in 4th ch from hook. Working down ch, 3 dc, 2 hdc, sc. Sl st in FL of next st of rnd 1, ch 2; rep from * twice, sl st in first st of rnd. Fasten off A.

Rnd 3: Join B with sl st in one of the ch-2 sp. Working in the free ch along the near side of the next petal, *3 sc, 2 hdc, ch 1, [(dc, ch 1, dc, ch 1) in next st)]] twice; [(dc, ch 1, dc, ch 1, dc, ch 1) in next ch] 3 times, [(dc, ch 1, dc, ch 1) in next st] twice, 2 hdc, 3 sc, sl st in the ch-2 sp; rep from * twice.

Rnd 4: Ch 1, *sl st 1 in first sc at base of next petal, ch 3, with the ch-3 across the RS of the petal, sl st in last sc of the same petal, ch 10, dc in 4th ch from hook, 3 dc, 2 hdc, sc. This is the beg of a tall petal; rep from * twice. Fasten off B if desired. Turn.

Rnd 5 (WS): Working in the opposite direction, continue with B or join C with sc in the first st of the tall petal, 2 sc, ch 1, (hdc, ch 1, hdc, ch 1) in next st, [(dc, ch 1, dc, ch 1) in next st] three times, (dc, ch 1, dc, ch 1) in each of the 3 ch around end of petal, [(dc, ch 1, dc, ch 1) in next st] 3 times, (hdc, ch 1, hdc, ch 1) in next st, 3 sc, PM in 8th and 16th ch-sp of this petal.

TINY PETAL
*Sl st in next ch-3 sp, (ch 3, 2 tr, ch 3, sc in 3rd ch from hook, 2 tr, ch 3, sl st) all in same ch-3 sp; remove hook from lp, insert hook from front to back in the first ch of this small petal, re-insert hook in free lp, pull lp through ch, ch 1 to anchor. **

2ND TALL PETAL
3 sc, ch 1, (hdc, ch 1, hdc, ch 1) in next st, [(dc, ch 1, dc, ch 1) in next st] twice, (dc, sl st in the ch-sp marked by the 2nd marker of the first petal, dc, ch 1) in next st, remove marker. (Dc, ch 1, dc, ch 1) in each of the 3 ch around end of petal, (dc,

FOR THESE FLOWERS WE USED

Lion Brand LB Collection Cotton Bamboo (52% cotton, 48% rayon from bamboo; 3.5oz/100g = 245yd/224m): (A) color Gardenia #170; (B) and (C) color Hyacinth #107; (D) color Snapdragon #174—light weight yarn;

GAUGE CIRCLE
(see page 11) = 1"/2.5cm worked on 4.00mm (size G-6 U.S.) hook

FINISHED MATERIALS
4¼"/10.8cm x 4⅝"/11.7cm (curled stem included)

Cascade Yarns Jewel Hand Dyed (100% wool; 3.5oz/100g = 142yd/129m): (A) color gold #9284; (B) color copper #9889; (C) color salmon #9283; (D) color green #9254—medium weight yarn;

GAUGE CIRCLE
(see page 11) = 1⅜"/3.5cm worked on 6.00mm (size J-10 U.S.) hook

FINISHED MATERIALS
4¾"/12cm x 6"/15.2cm (curled stem included)

Blue Sky Alpacas Alpaca Silk (50% alpaca, 50% silk; 1.75oz/50g = 146yd/133m): (A) color Mango #144; (B) color Brick #126; (C) color Quartz #101; (D) color Artichoke #131—fine weight yarn;

GAUGE CIRCLE
(see page 11) = ¾"/1.9cm worked on 3.50mm (size E-4 U.S.) hook

FINISHED MATERIALS
3½"/8.9cm x 3¾"/9.5cm (curled stem included)

ch 1, PM, dc, ch 1) in next st, [(dc, ch 1, dc, ch 1) in next st] twice, (hdc, ch 1, hdc, ch 1) in next st, 3 sc. PM in the 16th ch-sp of this petal.

Now you have a marker on each tall petal.

Rep between * and ** for the next tiny petal.

3RD TALL PETAL

3 sc, ch 1, (hdc, ch 1, hdc, ch 1) in next st, (dc, ch 1, dc, ch 1) in next st twice, [(dc, sl st in the ch-sp with the marker of the 2nd petal, dc, ch 1) in next st] remove marker. (Dc, ch 1, dc, ch 1) in each of the 3 ch around the end of this petal, (dc, ch 1, sl st in the ch-sp with the marker in the first

petal, dc, ch 1) in next st, remove marker. [(Dc, ch 1, dc, ch 1)in next st] twice, (hdc, ch 1, hdc, ch 1) in next st, 3 sc, sl st in next ch-3 sp.

Rep bet * and ** for the next tiny petal. Fasten off.

Greenery

Turn the flower upside down.

Rnd 1: Join D with sc in any BL of rnd 1, *(2 sc) in next st, sc; rep from * once, (2 sc) in last st—9 sc.

Rnds 2-4: Sc in each st around.

Rnd 5: (Sc, sc2tog) 3 times—6 sc. Stuff the green tube.

Rnd 6: Ch 1, pinch the tube flat, with the ch 1 at the fold. Sc2tog sts 1 and 6, sc2tog sts 2 and 5, sc2tog sts 3 and 4.

Stem

Ch 16, hdc in 3rd ch from hook, hdc in each rem ch, sl st in the sc2tog at the beg of rnd 6. Fasten off.

Finishing

Weave in ends. Do not block.

Sulfur Butterfly & Friends

Sulphur butterflies flit around the garden with wings ranging in color from a neon lemon yellow to a deep yellow-orange. Here are several variations, which you can dress up with embroidery or other embellishments.

SKILL LEVEL
Intermediate

MATERIALS & TOOLS
Up 3 colors of yarn of similar weight: butterfly colors (A, B, and C) used in any order

Hook: Appropriate size hook to achieve a firm gauge with selected yarn

Tapestry needle

PATTERN NOTE
In round 2, crochet in the free loops of the original chains, as well as in chains and regular stitches. If you have trouble orienting yourself, find the turning chain, then find the reference to the turning chain in the pattern. Count backward or forward to figure out where you are. When you dc in the 4th chain from the hook, you create a 3-st turning chain; a tr in the 5th chain from the hook creates a 4-st turning chain.

FOR THESE BUTTERFLIES WE USED
Berroco Ultra® Alpaca (50% super fine alpaca, 50% Peruvian wool; 3.5oz/100g = 215yd/198m): (A) color purple #6259 or tan #6214; (B) color red #6236; (C) color orange #6263 (used in different combinations)—light weight yarn;

GAUGE CIRCLE
(see page 11) = 1"/2.5cm worked on 4.00mm (size G-6 U.S.) hook

FINISHED MATERIALS
3"/7.6cm x 2½"/6.4cm (3-color variation is very slightly larger)

Cascade 220 Wool (100% Peruvian Highland wool; 3.5oz/100g = 220yd/200m): (A) color yellow #7828; (B) color yellow-green #8903; (C) color pale yellow #2439 (used in various combinations)—medium weight yarn;

INSTRUCTIONS
Simple Sulphur (see page 33)
Starting at a lower wing, with A, ch 6.

Rnd 1: Dc in 4th ch from hook, (hdc, sc) in next st, sc, ch 1, turn.

GAUGE CIRCLE
(see page 11) = 1"/2.9cm worked on 4.00mm (size G-6 U.S.) hook

FINISHED MATERIALS
3"/7.6cm x 2⅝"/6.7cm (3-color variation is very slightly larger)

SPECIAL ABBREVIATION

Hdc-sc-tog: Yo, insert hook in next stitch, yo and draw up a loop, insert hook in next st, yo and draw up a loop (4 loops on hook), yo and draw through remaining loops on hook.

Htr (half treble crochet): Yo 2 times, insert hook in stitch and draw up a loop (4 loops on hook), yo and draw through 2 loops (3 loops on hook), yo and draw through 3 loops (1 loop left on hook).

Sl st-picot: Ch 3, sl st in base of chain.

Upper wing: Sc, ch 8, turn and working back toward the center of the butterfly, tr in 5th ch from hook, htr, dc, hdc, sc in first sc of this wing.

Two Color
Variation

Three Color
Variation

2nd upper wing: Ch 9, turn and working back toward the center of the butterfly, tr in 5th ch from hook, htr, dc, hdc, sc. Sl st in the side of the sc between the first 2 wings, turn.

2nd lower wing: Sc in first st of previous row, ch 6, turn and working back toward the center of the butterfly, dc in 4th ch from hook, hdc-sc-tog, sc in the first sc of this wing, join to first st of rnd with sl st.

Rnd 2: Continue to work in the same direction, working around each wing, crocheting in the free ch lps on one edge of the wing, crocheting in each turning ch, and in the top of each st on the other edge of the wing.

First lower wing: (You already have a sl st join in the first st of this wing), sc, (2 hdc) in next st, (hdc, dc) in first st of turning ch, (2 dc) in next ch, (2 dc, hdc) in 3rd st of turning ch, hdc, sc, sl st.

First upper wing: Sk the st between the wings, and beg in the free lp of the first ch at the lower edge of the wing, 2 sl sts, sc, hdc, (2 hdc) in each of the first 2 sts of turning ch, (hdc, ch 1, dc, hdc) into 3rd st of turning ch, sc in 4th st of turning ch, 4 sc, sl st.

2nd upper wing: Sl st, 4 sc, sc in first st of turning ch, (hdc, dc, ch 1, hdc) in 2nd st of turning ch, (2 hdc) in each of next 2 sts of turning ch, hdc, sc, 2 sl sts.

2nd lower wing: Sk st between wings, sl st, sc, hdc, (hdc, 2 dc) in first st of turning ch, (2 dc) in next st of turning ch, (dc, hdc) in last st of turning ch, (2 hdc) in next st, sc, sl st, cut yarn and needle join to first st of rnd.

BODY
With color of your choice, ch 8, sl st in 2nd ch from hook, 4 sl sts, 2 sc, leaving a long tail for sewing, cut yarn and needle join to first ch of piece.

Two-Color Variation
Work through the end of rnd 1 in A, but do not join with sl st: instead, needle join to the first st of rnd. Join B with sl st in the needle joined st, which is the first st of rnd 1. Finish rnd 2 with B. Make a Body as above.

Three-Color Variation
Work through the end of rnd 1 in A, but do not join with sl st: instead, needle join to the first st of rnd.

Rnd 2:First lower wing: Join B with sl st in the needle joined stitch, which is the first st of rnd 1, 2 sl sts, (2 sc) in each of the 3 sts of turning ch, sc, 2 sl sts.

First upper wing: Sk st between wings, 3 sl sts, sc, sc in first st of turning ch, (2 sc) in next st, sc in 3rd st of turning ch, (2 sc) in next st, 5 sl sts.

2nd upper wing: 5 sl sts, (2 sc) in first st of turning ch, sc, (2 sc) in 3rd st of turning ch, sc in last st of turning ch, sc, 3 sl sts.

2nd lower wing: Sk st between wings, 2 sl sts, sc, (2 sc) in each of the 3 sts of turning ch, 3 sl sts, cut yarn and needle join to first st of rnd.

Rnd 3: Work in BL only all the way around.

First lower wing: Join C with sl st in the needle-joined stitch, which is the first st of rnd 2, sl st, 2 sc, (2 hdc) in next st, 2 hdc, (3 hdc) in next st, hdc, sc, 2 sl sts.

First upper wing: Sk 1 st, 3 sl sts, (2 sc) in each of the next 2 sts, 2 hdc, (hdc, dc, ch 1, hdc) in next st, 2 sc, 4 sl sts.

2nd upper wing: 4 sl sts, 2 sc, (hdc, ch 1, dc, hdc) in next st, 2 hdc, (2 sc) in each of next 2 sts, 3 sl sts.

2nd lower wing: Sk 1 st, 2 sl sts, sc, hdc, (3 hdc) in next st, 2 hdc, (2 hdc) in next st, 2 sc, 2 sl sts, cut yarn and needle join to first st of rnd.

Other Variations

For a pointy tip on the upper wings, replace the ch 1 at the corner of the wings with sl st-picot. Add buttons for "eye spots." Try different color combinations.

Finishing

Sew body to top of wings, centering it as shown, with the wide end of the body at the upper end of butterfly. Weave in ends, block. Add embellishments if desired.

For Wings with Painted Tips, See Other Variations

Simple Sulfur Butterfly

Coleus Leaf

Coleus leaves seem improbable with their pinks, purples, reds, and touches of green. Go for the coleus look by changing colors every row, or by crocheting the entire leaf in one variegated yarn.

Three Yarn
Coleus Leaf

SKILL LEVEL
Intermediate

MATERIALS & TOOLS
Up 3 colors of yarn of similar weight: leaf colors pink or red, purple, and green (A, B, and C) used in any order, or one variegated yarn

Hook: Appropriate size hook to achieve a firm gauge with selected yarn

Tapestry needle

SPECIAL ABBREVIATION
Sl st-picot: Ch 3, sl st in base of chain.

PATTERN NOTE
To make pattern-reading easier, the same leaf pattern is written for three yarn colors and for one yarn.

INSTRUCTIONS

Three Yarn Leaf
With A, ch 12.

Rnd 1: Dc2tog over the 5th and 6th ch from hook, 2 dc, 2 hdc, 2 sc. Ch 3, rotate the piece to work in the free lps on the other side of the original ch, 2 sc, 2 hdc, 2 dc, dc2tog, ch 4, sl st in same ch as last st. Fasten off A.

Rnd 2: Continuing in the same direction, join B with sl st in each of the first 2 ch of rnd 1. Working in FL only, (sl st-picot, sk 1 st, sl st in next st) 4 times, (sl st-picot, sk 1 st, sl st in next ch) 2 times, (sl st-picot, sk 1, sl st in next st) 4 times. Working into both lps, sl st-picot, sk 1, sl st in each of the last 2 ch of rnd 1. Cut yarn and needle join to first st of rnd.

Rnd 3: Join C with sc in BL of each of the first 2 sl sts of rnd 2. Working now in BL of rnd 1, hdc (this st will be behind the first sl st-picot of rnd 2), ch 1, (dc, ch 1, dc) in next st, ch 1, tr, ch 1, (sk 1 st, tr, ch 1) 3 times. Tr in the first ch of the ch-3 sp of rnd 1, ch 1, (tr, sl st-picot, tr) in the next ch, ch 1, tr in 3rd ch, ch 1, tr in next st. (Ch 1, sk 1 st, tr) 3 times, (dc, ch 1, dc) in next st, ch 1, hdc. Sc in BL of each of the last 2 sl sts of rnd 2.

To make stem, ch 6, sc in 2nd ch from hook, sl st in rem ch. Cut yarn and needle join to first st of rnd.

One Yarn Leaf
With variegated or solid color yarn, ch 12.

Rnd 1: Dc2tog over the 5th and 6th ch from hook. 2 dc, 2 hdc, 2 sc. Ch 3, rotate the piece to work in the free lps on the other side of the original ch. 2 sc, 2 hdc, 2 dc, dc2tog, ch 4, sl st in same ch as last st.

FOR THESE LEAVES WE USED

Berroco Origami™ (58% acrylic, 16% linen, 15% nylon, 11% cotton; 1.75oz/50g = 98yd/90m): (A, B, and C) color Cucumber Water #4360—medium weight yarn; (4)

GAUGE CIRCLE
(see page 11) = 1"/2.5cm worked on 4.00mm (size G-6 U.S.) hook

FINISHED MATERIALS
2¼"/5.7cm x 4"/10cm

Prism Pebbles (100% nylon; 2oz/56g = 123yd/112m): (A, B, and C) color Freesia--bulky weight yarn; (5)

GAUGE CIRCLE
(see page 11) = 1⅜"/3.5cm worked on 6.50mm (size K-10 ½ U.S.) hook

FINISHED MATERIALS
3"/7.5cm x 5⅛"/13cm

Cascade 220 Wool (100% Peruvian Highland wool; 3.5oz/100g = 220yd/200m): (A) color purple #7808; (B) color pinkish red #2428; (C) color green #7814—medium weight yarn; (4)

GAUGE CIRCLE
(see page 11) = 1"/2.5cm worked on 4.00mm (size G-6 U.S.) hook

FINISHED MATERIALS
2⅛"/5.4cm x 3¾"/9.5cm

One Yarn Coleus Leaf

Rnd 2: Sl st in each of the first 2 ch of rnd 1. Working in FL only, (sl st-picot, sk 1 st, sl st in next st) 4 times, (sl st-picot, sk 1 st, sl st in next ch) 2 times, (sl st-picot, sk 1, sl st in next st) 4 times. No longer working in FL only, sl st-picot, sk 1 st, sl st in each of the last 2 ch of rnd 1.

Rnd 3: Sc in BL of each of the first 2 sl sts of rnd 2. Working now in BL of rnd 1, hdc (this st will be behind the first sl st-picot of rnd 2), ch 1, (dc, ch 1, dc) in next st, ch 1, tr, ch 1, (sk 1 st, tr, ch 1) 3 times. Tr in the

first ch of the ch-3 sp of rnd 1, ch 1, (tr, sl st-picot, tr) in the next ch, ch 1, tr in 3rd ch, ch 1, tr in next st. (Ch 1, sk 1 st, tr) 3 times, (dc, ch 1, dc) in next st, ch 1, hdc. Sc in BL of each of the last 2 sl sts of rnd 2.

To make stem, ch 6, sc in 2nd ch from hook, sl st in remaining ch. Cut yarn and needle join to first st of rnd.

Finishing
Weave in ends, block.

Orchid

Orchids are an example of reality being stranger than fiction. They grow in many fantastic shapes and colors. This is one of the tamer varieties. Leave it plain, or dress it up with beads and embroidery.

SKILL LEVEL
Easy

MATERIALS & TOOLS
2 colors of yarn of similar weight: pink or white (A), deep pink or magenta (B)

Hook: Appropriate size hook to achieve a firm gauge with selected yarn

Optional: Seed and/or bugle beads, and sewing thread and needle to attach beads; or embroidery floss

Tapestry needle

SPECIAL ABBREVIATION
Htr (half treble crochet): Yo 2 times, insert hook in stitch and draw up a loop (4 loops on hook), yo and draw through 2 loops (3 loops on hook), yo and draw through 3 loops (1 loop left on hook).

INSTRUCTIONS
Back Petals
With A, ch 5, join with sl st in first ch to form a ring.

Rnd 1: Ch 1, working in ring, (sc, hdc, 2 dc, hdc) 3 times. Join with sl st to first sc of rnd.

FOR THESE FLOWERS WE USED
Cascade 220 Wool (100% Peruvian Highland wool; 3.5oz/100g = 220yd/200m): (A) color cream #8010 or pink #9477; (B) color magenta #8909 or 2428—medium weight yarn; (4)

GAUGE CIRCLE
(see page 11) = 1"/2.5cm worked on 4.00mm (size G-6 U.S.) hook

FINISHED MATERIALS
3¹⁄₁₆"/7.7cm x 2⅞"/7.3cm

Rnd 2: *(Sc, hdc) in hdc of rnd below, (dc, htr) in first dc, (htr, dc) in 2nd dc, (hdc, sc) in next hdc; rep from * twice.

Rnd 3: *Ch 1, sl st in sc of rnd below, sc in hdc, (hdc, dc) in dc, ch 1, (htr, tr) in first htr, (tr, htr) in 2nd htr, (dc, hdc) in dc, sc, sl st; rep from * twice. Fasten off.

Front Petals
With A, ch 5, join with sl st in first ch to form a ring.

Petal 1, Row 1 (RS): Ch 2, dc and hdc in ring; ch 2, turn.

Prism Kid Slique (66% rayon, 26% kid mohair, 8% nylon; 2oz/56g = 88yd/80m): (A) color Dune; (B) color Tea Rose—bulky weight yarn; (5)

Alternate (B) Prism Pebbles (100% nylon; 2oz/56g = 123yd/112m), (B) color Freesia—bulky weight yarn; (5)

GAUGE CIRCLE
(see page 11) = 1¼"/3cm worked on 5.00mm (size H-8 U.S.) hook

FINISHED MATERIALS
3¾"/9.5cm x 3⅝"/9.2cm

Petal 1, Row 2: (3 hdc) in first hdc, (2 dc) in dc, (4 hdc) in top st of turning ch; ch 1, turn.

Petal 1, Row 3: Sc, hdc, sc, (hdc, dc) in next st, (2 tr) in each of next 2 sts, (dc, hdc) in next st, sc, hdc, sc in top st of turning ch from last row. Working down the side of the petal, sl st in 2nd st of turning ch of last row, then sl st 2 in side of hdc from the first row. Sl st in ring.

Petal 2 (RS): Ch 2, 5 hdc in ring, ch 2, sl st in ring.

Petal 3: Work as for Petal 1. Fasten off, leaving a long tail for sewing.

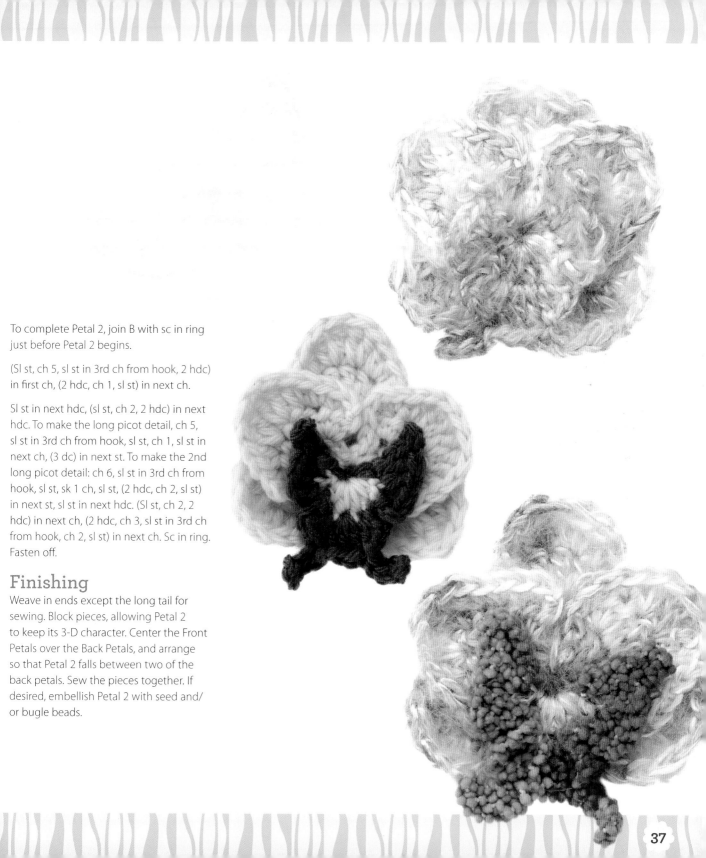

To complete Petal 2, join B with sc in ring just before Petal 2 begins.

(Sl st, ch 5, sl st in 3rd ch from hook, 2 hdc) in first ch, (2 hdc, ch 1, sl st) in next ch.

Sl st in next hdc, (sl st, ch 2, 2 hdc) in next hdc. To make the long picot detail, ch 5, sl st in 3rd ch from hook, sl st, ch 1, sl st in next ch, (3 dc) in next st. To make the 2nd long picot detail: ch 6, sl st in 3rd ch from hook, sl st, sk 1 ch, sl st, (2 hdc, ch 2, sl st) in next st, sl st in next hdc. (Sl st, ch 2, 2 hdc) in next ch, (2 hdc, ch 3, sl st in 3rd ch from hook, ch 2, sl st) in next ch. Sc in ring. Fasten off.

Finishing

Weave in ends except the long tail for sewing. Block pieces, allowing Petal 2 to keep its 3-D character. Center the Front Petals over the Back Petals, and arrange so that Petal 2 falls between two of the back petals. Sew the pieces together. If desired, embellish Petal 2 with seed and/ or bugle beads.

Violet & Violet Leaf

Fresh violets are good in salads or cold soups. Candied blossoms are used as garnishes for cakes and pastries. Think of crocheted violets as high-fiber garnish for your most delicious projects.

SKILL LEVEL
Intermediate

MATERIALS & TOOLS
2 colors of yarn of similar weight: violet color (A), leaf color (B)

Small amounts of white and yellow yarn for embroidery OR white and yellow paint OR white yarn and yellow beads

Hook: Appropriate size hook to achieve a firm gauge with selected yarn

Tapestry needle

SPECIAL ABBREVIATION
BPdc (Back Post double crochet): Yo, insert hook from back to front between the stitch you just finished and the next stitch. Push hook to the back between the next stitch and the stitch after that. At this point, you'll see your hook across the front of the next stitch, and the top of the stitch that you would normally crochet into (but not this time), is pushed toward you. Yo, draw up a loop, which will come around the front of the stitch, (yo, draw through 2 loops) twice.

INSTRUCTIONS

Flower

BACK PETALS
Row 1: *Ch 8, hdc in 4th ch from hook, dc, htr, dc, sl st; rep from * 3 more times, sl st in base of the beg ch-8 (4 petals). Fasten off and weave in ends.

FRONT PETAL
Row 1: Ch 10; yo, draw up a lp in the 3rd ch from hook, yo, sk next ch, draw up a lp in the next ch (5 lps on hook), (yo and draw through 2 lps on hook) 2 times, yo, draw through 3 lps on hook, tr, htr, dc, sc, sl st. Fasten off, leaving a long tail for sewing.

FINISHING
Pull long tail through the center of the Violet Back Petals. Arrange the Back Petals as you like and sew the Front Petal in place. Sew or paint white (or desired color) from the narrow end of the Violet

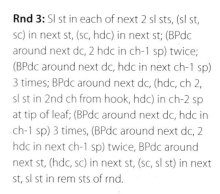

FOR THESE FLOWERS & LEAVES WE USED

Brown Sheep Company Lamb's Pride (85% wool, 15% mohair; 4oz/113g = 190yd/173m): (A) color Supreme Purple #M-100; (B) color Limeade #M-120—medium weight yarn; 🔘

GAUGE CIRCLE
(see page 11) = 1³⁄₁₆"/3cm worked on 5.00mm (size H-8 U.S.) hook

FINISHED MATERIALS
Flower 2⅝"/6.7cm x 3"/7.6cm; Leaf, excluding stem 3¼"/8.2cm x 3⅛"/8cm

DMC Satin (100% rayon; 8.7yd/8m): (A) color violet #S799, (B) color green #S47— embroidery floss; 🔘 (Please read section on working with slick yarns, page 00).

GAUGE CIRCLE
(see page 11) = ¹¹⁄₁₆"/1.8cm worked on 3.25mm (size 0 steel U.S.) hook

FINISHED MATERIALS
Flower 1¼"/3.2cm x 1⅜"/3.5cm; Leaf, excluding stem 1¾"/4.5cm x 1⅝"/4.1cm

Berroco Suede® (100% nylon; 1.75oz/50g = 120yd/111m): (A) Wyatt Earp #3755, (B) Aloe Vera #3786—medium weight yarn; 🔘

GUAGE CIRCLE
(see page 11) = 1"/2.5cm worked on 4.00mm (size G-6 U.S.) hook

FINISHED MATERIALS
Flower 2⅛"/5.4cm x 2½"/6.4cm; Leaf, excluding stem 2⅝"/6.7cm x 2 ¹¹⁄₁₆"/6.8cm

Front Petal, extending a little less than one-third across the petal. Add two yellow dots near the narrow end, either with paint, beads, or embroidered French knots. Weave in ends.

Leaf

Ch 4, join with sl st in first ch to form a ring.

Rnd 1: Ch 3, 2 dc, hdc, sc, dc, ch 1, dc, sc, hdc, 2 dc, ch 3, sl st in ring.

Rnd 2: Sl st in each of next 2 ch, (sc, hdc) in next ch, dc in first dc, ch 1, (dc, ch 1) 4 times; (dc, ch 2, dc) in ch-1 sp (this is the tip of the leaf); (ch 1, dc) 5 times, (hdc, sc) in next ch st, sl st in each rem ch st. Sc in ring.

Rnd 3: Sl st in each of next 2 sl sts, (sl st, sc) in next st, (sc, hdc) in next st; (BPdc around next dc, 2 hdc in ch-1 sp) twice; (BPdc around next dc, hdc in next ch-1 sp) 3 times; BPdc around next dc, (hdc, ch 2, sl st in 2nd ch from hook, hdc) in ch-2 sp at tip of leaf; (BPdc around next dc, hdc in ch-1 sp) 3 times, (BPdc around next dc, 2 hdc in next ch-1 sp) twice, BPdc around next st, (hdc, sc) in next st, (sc, sl st) in next st, sl st in rem sts of rnd.

MAKE STEM

Ch desired length between 15 and 30 sts. Sc in 2nd ch from hook, sl st in rem ch, needle join to first st of rnd 3.

FINISHING

Weave in ends.

For a violet plant arrangement, group the leaves so they seem to grow from a central point. Nestle the violets among the leaves, a little lower than the highest leaves. A flower stem should rise above the flower and curve back down to it.

Dogwood

Growing as they do under taller trees, blooming dogwoods look like pieces of lace hovering above the forest floor. Tiny dogwood flowers bloom from the green buds clustered in the center. The white or pink "petals" are really modified leaves.

SKILL LEVEL
Intermediate

MATERIALS & TOOLS
2 or 3 colors of yarn of similar weight: white or pink petal color (A), brown, green, or pink accent color for the ends of the petals (B), green center color (C)

Hook: Appropriate size hook to achieve a firm gauge with selected yarn

Piece of stiff card, approximately ½"/1.3cm x 3"/7.5cm

Tapestry needle

SPECIAL ABBREVIATIONS
Hdc-dc-htr-tog: Yo, insert hooks in next stitch, yo and draw up a loop, yo and insert hook in the next st, yo and draw up a loop, yo, draw through 2 loops on hook, yo twice and insert hook in the next st, yo and draw up a loop (7 loops on hook), yo and draw through 2 loops, yo and draw through remaining loops on hook.

Htr (half treble crochet): Yo 2 times, insert hook in stitch and draw up a loop (4 loops on hook), yo and draw through 2 loops (3 loops on hook), yo and draw through 3 loops (1 loop left on hook).

Htr-dc-tog: Yo twice, insert hook in next stitch, yo and draw up a loop, yo and draw through 2 lps, yo and insert hook in the next st, yo and draw up a loop (5 loops on hook), yo and draw through 2 loops, yo and draw through remaining loops on hook.

Tr2tog: Treble crochet 2 stitches together

PATTERN NOTE
When you remove the hook from a loop, prevent the loop from unraveling by expanding the loop or by inserting a safety pin or split ring marker in the loop. It's easiest just to expand the loop.

FOR THESE FLOWERS WE USED
Prism Symphony (80% merino, 10% cashmere, 10% nylon; 2oz/56g = 118yd/107m): (A) color Antique or Sunrise; (B) color Sunrise or Moss; (C) color Moss—medium weight yarn; [4]

GAUGE CIRCLE
(see page 11) = 1"/2.5cm worked on 4.00mm (size G-6 U.S.) hook

FINISHED MATERIALS
3¾"/9.5cm with petals still a little curled

Blue Sky Alpacas Skinny Dyed (100% organically grown cotton; 2.3oz/65g = 150yd/137m): (A) color Pink #305; (B) color Coral #317—light weight yarn; [3]

Center is the Pasque Flower center worked with No. 10 crochet cotton and a 2.00mm (size 4 steel U.S.) hook

GAUGE CIRCLE
(see page 11) = 15⁄16"/2.4cm worked on 4.00mm (size G-6 U.S.) hook

FINISHED MATERIALS
3¾"/9.5cm

INSTRUCTIONS

Flower

With A, ch 4, join with sl st in first ch to form a ring.

Row 1(RS): Ch 12. Hdc-dc-htr-tog across the 3rd, 4th, and 5th ch from hook, tr, tr2tog, htr-dc-tog, hdc, sc, ch 1, turn.

Row 2: Continuing with A, lay accent color B along the row, and crochet over it so it is hidden inside the sts, sc, 2 hdc, dc. Remove the hook from the last st (see Pattern Note). Turn to RS of the petal, find the st of row 1 where you inserted the hook for the dc of this row. Now move to the next st along, and insert hook in that st, yo with B, pull lp through st. With B, 2 sl sts in the lps on the side of the last dc (NOT around the st, but in it). Drop the B yarn at the WS of petal. Insert hook back into the A lp that you left free earlier in the row—2 lps on hook.

Row 3: With A, ch 1, pulling the yarn through the A lp and the B lp, (1 lp rem on hook). Continuing with A, ch 3, (hdc, dc, htr) all in 3rd ch from hook, tr in next A-colored ch (avoid the B-colored lp). Lay the B yarn along the row and crochet over it as before, (2 tr) in next st, (htr, dc) in next st, hdc, sc, sl st in ring. Drop B yarn for now.

Rep rows 1-3 three times. Fasten off.

Flower Center

Cut a 10"/25cm length of A, thread into tapestry needle, and set aside. Wrap C about 15 times around the piece of card, but do not cut yarn yet. Slide the tapestry needle under the wraps and draw A under the wraps, centering its length. Use the tails of A to tie a simple overhand knot around the wraps. Slide the card out of the wraps. Pull the knot tighter and tie the tails again to lock the knot in place. Now cut C. Arrange and fluff the loops to make a nice center. Use the tails of A to sew the center to the Dogwood flower. Trim the C ends and hide them among the loops.

Finishing

Weave in ends. Block gently, allowing the petal ends to curl a little. Sew flower center in place.

Pineapple

Columbus sailed the ocean blue and brought home Europe's first pineapple. Hosts went to great trouble to serve the delicious new fruit to their appreciative guests. That's probably how the pineapple became a symbol of welcome and hospitality.

SKILL LEVEL
Easy

MATERIALS & TOOLS
2 colors of yarn of similar weight: gold or brown (A), green (B)

Hook: Appropriate size hook to achieve a firm gauge with selected yarn

Tapestry needle

Blocking supplies

SPECIAL ABBREVIATION
Lp picot (loop picot): (sl st, ch 3, sl st) in same st or sp.

FOR THESE FRUITS WE USED

Caron International Naturally Caron Country (25% merino wool, 75% microdenier acrylic; 3oz/85g = 185yd/170m): (A) color Spice House #0018; (B) color Loden Forest #0020—medium weight yarn; (4)

GAUGE CIRCLE
(see page 11) = 1"/2.5cm worked on 4.00mm (size G-6 U.S.) hook in A

FINISHED MATERIALS
4"/10cm x 5⅝"/14cm

Berroco Ultra® Alpaca (50% super fine alpaca, 50% Peruvian wool; 3.5oz/100g = 215yd/198m): (A) color yellow #6225; (B) color green #6273—light weight yarn; (3)

GAUGE CIRCLE
(see page 11) = 1"/2.5cm worked on 4.00mm (size G-6 U.S.) hook

FINISHED MATERIALS
4¼"/11cm x 5¼"/13cm

INSTRUCTIONS

Cone

Row 1 (RS): With A, ch 15, lp picot in 6th ch from hook, (ch 5, sk 2 ch, lp picot in next ch) twice, ch 2, sk 2 ch, sl st in last ch, turn.

Row 2: (Ch 5, lp picot in next ch-5 sp) twice, ch 5, sl st in the ch-sp at end of previous row, ch 6, turn.

Row 3: (Lp picot in next ch-5 sp, ch 5) twice, lp picot in next ch-5 sp, ch 2, tr in sl st at end of row 2.

Row 4: Rep row 2.

Row 5: (Lp picot in next ch-5 sp, ch 5) twice, lp picot in next ch-5 sp, ch 2, tr in top of tr of row below.

Rows 6 and 7: Rep rows 4 and 5.

Row 8: (Ch 5, lp picot in next ch-5 sp) twice, ch 2, dc in ch-sp at end of previous row.

Row 9: Ch 1, sl st in ch-2 sp, (ch 3, sl st in next ch-5 sp) twice, ch 1.

Border rnd (RS): Working down side of pineapple, 2 sc in same ch-sp, (3 sc around next tr) 3 times, (sc, 3 hdc) in ch-sp at bottom corner.

Working across the bottom, (3 hdc in next ch-sp) twice, (3 hdc, sc) in ch-sp at corner.

Working up the other side of the pineapple, (3 sc in next ch-sp) 3 times, 2 sc around dc.

Across the top of the pineapple, (3 hdc in next ch-3 sp) twice. Fasten off and needle-join to first sc of rnd.

Leaves

Row 1: Join B with sc in the first hdc at the top of the pineapple (about 6 sts back from where you ended A). Ch 11, sl st in 4th ch from hook. Working down the ch, sc, hdc, dc, (2 dc) in next st, 3 dc. Sk 1 hdc of previous rnd, sc in next hdc. Ch 13, sl st in 4th ch from hook. Working down the ch, sc, hdc, 7 dc. Sk 1 hdc of previous rnd, sc in next hdc. Ch 12, sl st in 4th ch from hook. Working down the ch, sk 1 ch, sc, hdc, dc, (dc2tog) twice. Sk 1 hdc of previous rnd, sc in next sc, ch 1. Turn to WS of pineapple.

Row 2: You'll be working in skipped sts on the last row. Sc in first skipped st. (Ch 12, sl st in 4th ch from hook. Working down ch, sc, hdc, 6 dc, sc in next skipped st) twice. Fasten off.

Finishing

Weave in ends. Stretch the cone lengthwise and across its width, several times, to even out the crocheted grid. Pin each leaf separately and use at least 4 pins to pin the fruit to your blocking surface. Block with steam.

Mini, Midi, & Maxi-Mums

Lots of easy-to-make petals fill out these plump mums. A little stuffing, held in by a crocheted back, holds their shape and makes them easier to attach to your projects.

SKILL LEVEL
Easy

MATERIALS & TOOLS
1 color of yarn: mum color (A)

Hook: Appropriate size hook to achieve a firm gauge with selected yarn

Stuffing

Tapestry needle

PATTERN NOTE
Change petal color or end the flower after any even-numbered row.

FOR THESE FLOWERS WE USED

Ivy Brambles SockScene (100% superwash merino; 4oz/113g = 410yd/378m): (A) color Dayglow #108 or Buttercup #106; optional (B) Sunrise #008—sock weight yarn;

GAUGE CIRCLE
(see page 11) = ¾"/1.9cm worked on 3.25mm (size 0 steel U.S.) hook

FINISHED MATERIALS
2⅜"/6cm (midi-mum); 2¹³⁄₁₆"/7.2cm (maxi-mum)

Spud and Chloë Fine (80% superwash wool, 20% silk; 2.3oz/65g = 248yd/227m): (A) color coral #7810—sock weight yarn;

GAUGE CIRCLE
(see page 11) = ¹¹⁄₁₆"/1.7cm worked on 3.25mm (size 0 steel U.S.) hook

FINISHED MATERIALS
1⁹⁄₁₆"/4cm (mini-mum)

INSTRUCTIONS

Mini-mum

Ch 5, join with sl st in first ch to form a ring.

Rnd 1: Ch 1, 10 sc in ring, join with sl st in the front lp of the first sc of rnd—10 sc.

Rnd 2: Working in FL only, *(sl st, ch 3, tr, ch 3, sl st) in the next st, sk 1 st (petal made); rep from * 4 times. After the last petal, do not sk 1 st, but join with sl st in

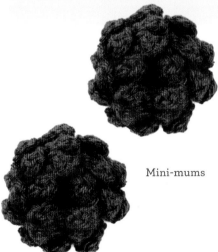

Mini-mums

BL of next sc, ch 1 and make the first st of the next rnd in the same st as the sl st—5 petals.

Rnd 3: Working in BL of rnd 1, *sc, (2 sc) in next st, 2 sc, (2 sc) in next st; rep from * once. Join with sl st in FL of first st of rnd—14 sc.

Rnd 4: Work as for rnd 2, except rep from * 6 times—7 petals.

Rnd 5: Working in BL of rnd 3, *sc, (2 sc) in next st, sc, (2 sc) in next st, 2 sc, (2 sc) in next st; rep from * once. Join with sl st in FL of first st of rnd—20 sc.

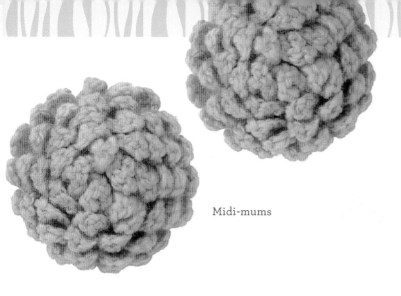

Midi-mums

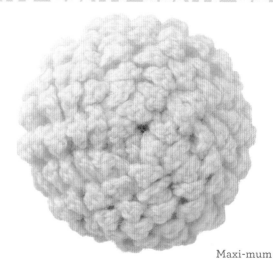

Maxi-mum

Rnd 6: Work as for rnd 2, except rep from * 9 times—10 petals. For the Mini-mum, fasten off.

Midi-mum

Rnds 1-6: Follow instructions for the Mini-mum, rnds 1-6, only do not fasten off after rnd 6.

Rnd 7: Working in BL of rnd 5, *sc, (2 sc) in next st, 2 sc, (2 sc) in next st; rep from * 3 times. Join with sl st in FL of first st of rnd—28 sc.

Rnd 8: Work as for rnd 2, except rep from * 13 times—14 petals.

Rnd 9: Working in BL of rnd 7, *2 sc, (2 sc) in next st, 3 sc, (2 sc) in next st; rep from * 3 times. Join with sl st in FL of first st of rnd—36 sc.

Rnd 10: Work as for rnd 2, except rep from * 17 times—18 petals. For the Midi-mum, fasten off.

Maxi-mum

Rnds 1-10: Follow instructions for the Mini-mum, rnds 1-6, only do not fasten off after rnd 6. Then follow instructions for the Midi-mum, rnds 7-10, only do not fasten off after rnd 10.

Rnd 11: Working in BL of rnd 9, *5 sc, (2 sc) in next st; rep from * 5 times—42 sc.

Rnd 12: Work as for rnd 2, except rep from * 20 times—21 petals.

Rnd 13: Working in BL of rnd 11, *6 sc, (2 sc) in next st; rep from * 5 times—48 sc.

Rnd 14: Work as for rnd 2, except rep from * 23 times—24 petals.

Fasten off.

Back for Mini-mum

With A, ch 5, join with sl st in first ch to form a ring.

Rnd 1: Ch 2, 9 hdc in ring. Join with sl st to top of ch-2 at beg of rnd. Fasten off, leaving a long tail for sewing.

Back for Midi-mum

With A, ch 5, join with sl st in first ch to form a ring.

Rnd 1: Ch 2, 11 hdc in ring. Join with sl st to top of ch-2 at beg of rnd.

Rnd 2: Ch 1, (2 sc) in each st around, join with sl st to first st of rnd—24 sc.

Rnd 3: Ch 1, *sc, (2 sc) in next st; rep from * 11 times, join with sl st to first st of

rnd—36 sc. Fasten off, leaving a long tail for sewing.

Back for Maxi-mum

With A, ch 5, join with sl st in first ch to form a ring.

Rnd 1: Ch 2, 11 hdc in ring. Join with sl st to top of ch-2 at beg of rnd.

Rnd 2: Ch 2 (counts as 1 hdc), hdc in same sp as ch, (2 hdc) in each rem st around, join with sl st to first st of rnd—24 hdc.

Rnd 3: Ch 1, *sc, (2 sc) in next st; rep from * 11 times, join with sl st to first st of rnd—36 sc.

Rnd 4: Ch 1, *2 sc, (2 sc) in next st; rep from * 11 times, join with sl st to first st of rnd. Fasten off, leaving a long tail for sewing.

Finishing

Notice that the back of the flower is a dome shape. Sew flower back to the back of the flower, hiding yarn ends inside and leaving a gap to push in stuffing. Use just enough stuffing to support the flower dome. Finish sewing flower back to flower. Weave in ends. Do not block.

Pincushion Mum

Whether hanging from your sewing machine or lying on your work table, this mum makes a great pincushion. The decorative oak leaves won't curl, because they are sewn back-to-back.

SKILL LEVEL
Intermediate

FINISHED MEASUREMENTS
2¾"/7cm x 3¼"/8.3cm (including leaf)

MATERIALS & TOOLS
Ellen's ½ Pint Farm Bella Sorella Sock Yarn (75% merino, 25% nylon; 3.5oz/100g = 440yd/400m): (A) color Reds; (B) color Rainbow—superfine weight yarn; **1**

Crochet hook: 3.25mm (size 0 steel U.S.) or size to obtain gauge

Light cardboard

Circular template, such as a small lid

Pen

Scissors to cut cardboard

Fabric glue

Heavy book for pressing

Stuffing

Tapestry needle

GAUGE CIRCLE
(see page 11) = 11/16"/1.7cm worked on 3.25mm (size 0 steel U.S.) hook'

INSTRUCTIONS

Flower

With A, make the Maxi-mum (page 44) and its back.

Place the back piece on the cardboard and trace around it, to give you an idea of its size. Then find a small lid or other circular template that fits inside your tracing, with about ⅛"/3mm leeway all around. Trace around the template. Cut along the newly traced line. The resulting circular piece of cardboard should fit on the crocheted back of the mum, with the last row sticking out beyond the edge of the cardboard. Trim the cardboard if necessary, keeping it as circular as possible.

Spread fabric glue onto cardboard and press the crocheted back into the glue. Adjust as needed. Press the glued piece under a heavy book and let dry.

Leaf

With B, make two Small Gambel Oak Leaves (page 21), leaving off the stems. Place leaves back to back and sew them together as invisibly as possible.

Hanging Loop

With A, ch 16, sc in 2nd ch from hook, sc in each rem ch st. Fasten off, leaving a long tail for sewing.

Finishing

Block only the outside petal round of the mum, so the petals do not curl as much as the other petals.

Sew crocheted back to the back of the mum, with the cardboard piece to the inside. Push stuffing between the pieces before you finish sewing.

Arrange the leaf so it peeks from behind the mum; sew in place.

Sew hanging loop to the edge of the back piece, close to the leaf.

Weave in ends.

Leafy Muffler

Gambel Oak leaves dress up this particular recycled sweater muffler, but you can use any leaves or flowers you want. Don't have an old sweater to recycle? Use a purchased scarf instead.

SKILL LEVEL
Intermediate

FINISHED MEASUREMENTS
Varies, depending upon choice of recyclable sweater and crocheted leaves

MATERIALS & TOOLS
Berroco Ultra® Alpaca (50% super fine alpaca, 50% Peruvian wool; 3.5oz/100g = 215yd/198m): (A) color Irwyn Green Mix #6273—light weight yarn;

Crochet hook: 4.00mm (size G-6 U.S.) or size to obtain gauge

Purchased scarf or muffler, or hand-wash only woolen sweater to recycle

Washing machine

Tapestry needle

Sewing thread and needle

GAUGE CIRCLE
(see page 11) = 1"/2.5cm worked on 4.00mm (size G-6 U.S.) hook

INSTRUCTIONS

Muffler

Open the seams on each side of the sweater and under the arms. If you're lucky, they will have been held together with a chain stitch; if you snip the correct end of it, it will zip out very easily. If moths have made holes in the sweater, close up the holes with a few stitches of yarn—no fancy darning necessary—just close the holes.

Wash the sweater in warm water with other laundry in your washing machine. Tumble dry for a few minutes only. We're taking this slowly, because we want a soft, pliable muffler.

Make a test cut at the armpit of the sweater. If the fulling process has worked, the sweater will have a fuzzy look and the stitches will not unravel. If the stitches do unravel, check the fiber content of the sweater again to make sure it is non-washable wool, then wash again in warm water.

When the sweater is fulled, cut same-width pieces for the muffler from the center of the sleeves, and the front and back of the sweater. It's up to you whether to include ribbing. You may be able to cut two pieces each from the front and back.

With the sweater leftovers, practice overlapping cut edges and sewing them together with yarn and a running stitch. Practice sewing a running stitch all around the edge of the piece. Wash again in cold water, block while still damp, let dry. Does it look fine? If not, do another practice run.

Alright, now do the real thing. Sew the ends of the muffler pieces together, sew a running stitch all around the muffler, wash in cold water with other laundry, block, and let dry.

Leaves

With A, make 2 small Gambel Oak Leaves and 3 large Gambel Oak Leaves (page 21), or desired number of leaves. Weave in ends and block.

Finishing

Arrange the leaves on the muffler as desired and pin them in place.

Sew with sewing thread down the middle of the leaf, into the stem, then around the outside of the leaf, leaving some of the lobe ends free to curl a little.

Welcome Guest Towels

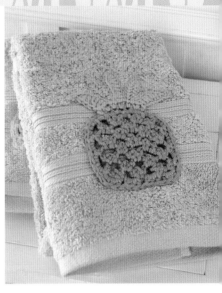

Pineapples crocheted with cotton yarn will wash (and dry!) right along with your guest towels.

SKILL LEVEL
Easy

FINISHED MEASUREMENTS
Varies depending on towel size

MATERIALS & TOOLS
Cascade Pima Tencel (50% Peruvian cotton, 50% tencel; 1.75oz/50g = 109yd/99m): (A) color tan #7101 or golden yellow #0258; (B) color green #9500—light weight yarn;

Crochet hook: 4.00mm (size G-6 U.S.) or size to obtain gauge

Purchased hand towel

Measuring tape

Pins

Sewing thread and needle

Tapestry needle

GAUGE CIRCLE
Gauge Circle (see page 11) = 1⁵⁄₁₆"/2.4cm worked on 4.00mm (size G-6 U.S.) hook

INSTRUCTIONS

Crochet a Pineapple (page 42) for each towel, weave in ends, and block as instructed in pattern.

Finishing

Place the Pineapple at one end of the towel, centered side-to-side, as in photo. Measure to make sure it is in the middle.

Pin in place.

Sew all around the edge, including the edges of the leaves. Make a stitch at the base of each loop picot in the body of the fruit. You can probably bury the sewing stitches in the thickness of the towel, but use a sewing thread that matches the towel, in case any stitches show on the back.

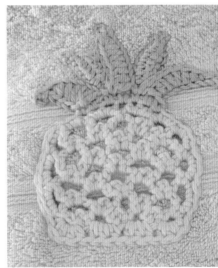

Inspired Garden

Pomegranate

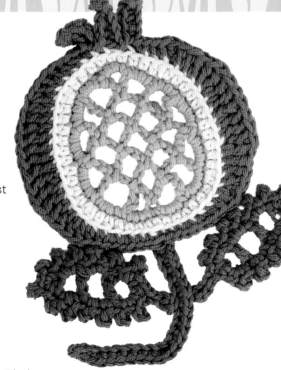

When we learned the story of Persephone in elementary school, our teacher brought a pomegranate for us to taste. It was my first experience with the tart, seedy fruit, which has been the subject of myth, symbolism, and needlework for many generations.

SKILL LEVEL
Experienced

MATERIALS & TOOLS
4 colors of yarn of similar weight: light orange or seed color (A), cream or pith color (B), dark orange or red or peel color (C), and greenery color (D)

Hook: Appropriate size hook to achieve a firm gauge with selected yarn

2 stitch markers

Tapestry needle

SPECIAL ABBREVIATIONS
Hdc2tog: Half double crochet 2 stitches together

Htr (half treble crochet): Yo 2 times, insert hook in stitch and draw up a loop (4 loops on hook), yo and draw through 2 loops (3 loops on hook), yo and draw through 3 loops (1 loop left on hook).

Sl st-picot: Ch 3, sl st in base of chain.

INSTRUCTIONS
Pomegranate

SEEDS OR CENTERPIECE
Using seed color (A), ch 12. PM in 6th ch from hook.

Row 1: Sl st in 9th ch from hook, ch 5, sk 2 ch, sl st in next ch, turn.

Row 2: Ch 8, PM in the 6th ch from hook, sl st in ch-5 sp of previous row, ch 5, sl st in next ch-sp of previous row, ch 5, dc in st with marker from previous row. Remove marker. Turn.

Row 3: Ch 6, sl st in ch-5 sp of previous row, (ch 5, sl st in next ch-sp) twice, ch 3, htr in marked st of previous row. Remove marker. Turn.

Row 4: (Ch 5, sl st in next ch-5 sp of previous row) twice, ch 5, sl st in ch-6 sp. Turn.

Row 5: Ch 7, sl st in ch-5 sp of previous row, (ch 5, sl st in next ch-sp) twice, ch 2, htr in top of the htr of row 3. Turn.

Row 6: (Ch 5, sl st in next ch-5 sp) twice, ch 3, dc in the ch-7 sp of previous row. Turn.

Row 7: Ch 5, sl st in next ch-5 sp, ch 2, dc in the next ch-5 sp. Turn.

Row 8: Ch 3, sl st in next ch-5 sp. Ch 1, continue working in the same direction.

Final Seed Rnd: Working down the side of the centerpiece, (3 sc) in the same ch-sp as sl st you just completed, (3 sc) in next sp, (4 sc in next sp) 3 times.

FOR THESE FRUITS WE USED

Brown Sheep Company Cotton Fleece, (80% cotton, 20% merino wool; 3.5oz/100g = 215yd/197m): (A) color Wild Orange #CW310, (B) color Cotton Ball #CW100, (C) color Barn Red #CW201, (D) color Holly Green #CW470—medium weight yarn; (4)

GAUGE CIRCLE
(see page 11) = 1⅛"/2.8cm worked on 5.00mm (size H-8 U.S.) hook

FINISHED MEASUREMENTS
5½"/14cm x 9¼"/23.5cm

Coats & Clark's Aunt Lydia's Classic Crochet Thread, No. 10, Art. 154 (100% mercerized cotton, 350yd/320m): (A) color Pumpkin #431, (B) color Cream #420, (C) color Victory Red #494, (D) color Wasabi Green #397—10-count crochet thread; (0)

GAUGE CIRCLE
(see page 11) = ⅜"/0.9cm worked on 2.00mm (size 4 steel U.S.) hook

FINISHED MEASUREMENTS
3"/7.6cm x 4¼"/10.8cm

Working across base of the centerpiece, (3 sc) in next sp, sc in next ch (which already has a st), PM in the finished st, (3 sc) in next sp.

Working up the other side of the centerpiece, (4 sc in next sp) 3 times, (3 sc in next sp) twice.

3 sc in ch-sp at top of centerpiece. Cut yarn and needle join to first st of rnd—7 sc across base, 18 sc on each side, 3 sc across top.

POMEGRANATE PITH

Turn centerpiece so you are looking at its base. Join pith color (B) with sc in st with a marker. Remove marker, 3 sc.

Working up the side of the centerpiece, 3 hdc, (2 hdc) in next st, 10 hdc, (2 hdc) in next st, 3 hdc.

3 sc across top.

Working down the other side of centerpiece, 3 hdc, (2 hdc) in next st, 10 hdc, (2 hdc) in next st, 3 hdc.

Finishing lower edge, 3 sc. Cut yarn and needle join to first st of rnd—7 sc across base, 20 hdc on each side, 3 sc across top.

Leaves at base of Pomegranate (make 2)
Ch 12.

Rnd 1: Sc in 3rd ch from hook, (ch 2, sk 2, dc in next st) twice, ch 2, sk 2, sc in next st, ch 1. Rotate leaf so you can crochet in the ch-sp formed by the original ch-12.

Rnd 2: *(Sc, sl st-picot, sc, sl st-picot) all in next ch-sp; rep from * twice. In the ch-sp at tip of the leaf, (sc, sl st-picot, sc), **(sl st-picot, sc, sl st-picot, sc) all in next ch sp; rep from ** twice.

To make the leaf stem, ch 5, sc in 2nd ch from hook, sl st in each of rem ch. Needle join to first st of rnd 2.

Curved Pomegranate Stem (optional)
Ch 20, sc in 2nd ch from hook, sc, (2 sc) in next st, *5 sc, (2 sc) in next st; rep from * once, 4 sc. Fasten off.

Finishing
Weave in ends. Sew stem to base of the pomegranate, and leaves at the base of the pomegranate and to the stem, as in photo.

POMEGRANATE PEEL
This rnd is worked in BL only of the previous rnd. Join peel color (C) with a sc in BL of first st of the previous rnd, 2 sc, (2 sc) in next st.

Working up the side, (2 sc) in next st, 2 hdc, (2 dc) in next st, dc, 2 htr, (2 tr) in next st, 4 tr, (2 tr) in next st, 2 htr, dc, (2 dc) in next st, 2 hdc, (2 sc) in next st.

TOPKNOT
Ch 6, sl st in 3rd ch from hook; working down ch, (2 hdc) in next st, hdc, sc, sl st in next st of previous rnd.

Ch 7, sl st in 3rd ch from hook; working down ch, sc, hdc, dc, hdc, sk 1 st of previous rnd, and sl st in next st.

Ch 7, sl st in 3rd ch from hook; working down ch, hdc2tog, hdc, sc.

Working down the other side, (2 sc) in next st, 2 hdc, (2 dc) in next st, dc, 2 htr, (2 tr) in next st, 4 tr, (2 tr) in next st, 2 htr, dc, (2 dc) in next st, 2 hdc, (2 sc) in next st.

Working across the bottom, (2 sc) in next st, 2 sc. Needle join to first st of rnd. Fasten off—9 sc across base, 26 sts on each side, topknot has three spikes.

Crescent Moonflower

The Moonflower's unfurling bud is a tiny replica of the swirling arms of galaxies in the night sky. In this crocheted version, you attach the petals to each other as you go.

SKILL LEVEL
Intermediate

MATERIALS & TOOLS
2 colors of yarn of similar weight: flower color (A), center color (B)

Hook: Appropriate size hook to achieve a firm gauge with selected yarn

Tapestry needle

SPECIAL ABBREVIATIONS
Htr (half treble crochet): Yo 2 times, insert hook in stitch and draw up a loop (4 loops on hook), yo and draw through 2 loops (3 loops on hook), yo and draw through 3 loops (1 loop left on hook).

Join-picot: Ch 1, join with sl st to indicated st, ch 1, sl st to first ch to complete picot.

Sl st-picot: Ch 3, sl st in base of chain.

FOR THESE FLOWERS WE USED

Tapetes de Lana Mill (Mora, NM) Cotswold Wool Yarn (100% wool): (A) color indigo-dyed, (B) color natural (also the other way around)—medium weight yarn; **(4)**

GAUGE CIRCLE
(see page 11) = 1¹⁄₁₆"/2.7cm worked on 5.00mm (size H-8 U.S.) hook

FINISHED MEASUREMENTS
4¾"/12.1cm

Malabrigo Silky Merino (50% silk, 50% baby merino wool; 1.75oz/50g = 150yd/137m): (A and B) color Caribeno #474—light weight yarn; **(3)**

GAUGE CIRCLE
(see page 11) = ⅞"/2.2cm worked on 4.00mm (size G-6 U.S.) hook

FINISHED MEASUREMENTS
3½"/8.9cm

INSTRUCTIONS

Flower
With A, ch 4, join with sl st in first ch to form a ring.

Row 1: Ch 1, (sl st-picot, ch 1) 8 times, ch 4, turn.

Row 2: Sl st in 5th ch from hook, ch 1, sk picot, sc in next ch, ch 1, sk picot, hdc in next ch, ch 1, sk picot, dc in next ch, (sk picot, htr in next ch) twice, sk picot, dc in next ch, ch 1, sk picot, hdc in next ch, ch 1, sk picot, sc in next ch, ch 1, sc in ring.

Row 3: Ch 1, (sl st-picot, ch 1) twice, join-picot in ch-5 sp at tip of previous petal, ch 1, (sl st-picot, ch 1) 5 times, ch 4, turn.

Rows 4-7: Rep rows 2 and 3 twice.

Row 8: Rep row 2.

Row 9: Ch 1, (sl st-picot, ch 1) twice, join-picot in ch-5 sp at tip of previous petal, ch 1, (sl st-picot, ch 1) 5 times, ch 1, sl st in 3rd picot of row 1, ch 2, turn.

Row 10: Sl st in ch just before the first picot, ch 1, sk picot, sc in next ch, ch 1, sk picot, hdc in next ch, ch 1, sk picot, dc in next ch, (sk picot, htr in next ch) twice, sk picot, dc in next ch, ch 1, sk picot, hdc in next ch, ch 1, sk picot, sc in next ch, ch 1, cut yarn and needle join to first sc of first petal.

Center
Ch 5, join with sl st in first ch to form a ring.

Rnd 1: Ch 1, (sc, hdc, dc, hdc) in ring 5 times, cut yarn and needle join to first sc of rnd.

Finishing
Sew Center to center of flower. Weave in ends, block.

Curly Ray Sunflower

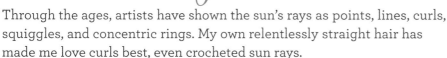

Through the ages, artists have shown the sun's rays as points, lines, curls, squiggles, and concentric rings. My own relentlessly straight hair has made me love curls best, even crocheted sun rays.

SKILL LEVEL
Intermediate

MATERIALS & TOOLS
1 to 5 colors of yarn of similar weight: center color (A), up to 3 optional center colors, petal color (B)

Hook: Appropriate size hook to achieve a firm gauge with selected yarn

Tapestry needle

SPECIAL ABBREVIATION
3 dc-CL: (Yo, insert hook in indicated st, yo, draw up a lp, yo, draw through 2 lps on hook) 3 times, yo, draw through all lps on hook, ch 1 to close the CL.

PATTERN NOTE
If you decide to make the flower center (rnds 1-4) in more than one color, end the round with a sl st or needle join and join the next color with the first st of the next round.

INSTRUCTIONS

Flower

With A, ch 6, join with sl st in first ch to form a ring.

Rnd 1: Ch 2, (yo, insert hook in ring, yo, draw up a loop, yo, draw through 2 lps) 2 times. Yo, draw through all loops on hook. First CL complete. Ch 2, *3dc-CL in ring, ch 2; rep from * 4 times. Join with sl st to the top of the first CL—6 dc-CL separated by 2 ch.

Rnd 2: Ch 1, *sc in top of CL, 3 sc in ch-sp; rep from * 5 times. Join with sl st to first sc of rnd—24 sc.

Rnd 3: Ch 2, (yo, insert hook in same st as sl st join of the last rnd, yo, draw up a lp, yo, draw through 2 lps) 2 times. Yo, draw through all lps on hook—first CL complete. Ch 2, sk 1 st, *3dc-CL in next st, ch 2, sk 1 st; rep from * 10 times. Join with sl st in top of the first CL—12 dc-CL separated by 2 ch.

Rnd 4: Ch 1, *sc in top of CL, 3 sc in ch-sp; rep from * 11 times. Join with sl st to first sc of rnd—48 sc. Fasten off.

Rnd 5 (petal rnd): With B, join with sl st in any sc of rnd 4. Ch 8, (3 sc) in 2nd ch from hook, (2 sc, hdc) in next ch, (3 hdc) in next ch, (hdc, 2 dc) in next ch, dc, htr, tr. Sk 3 sts of rnd 4, sl st in next st. First petal complete.

Petals 2-11: Ch 8, (3 sc) in 2nd ch from hook. Join to previous petal as follows: working the 3 sts in the parentheses all into next ch: (sc, keeping the ch and yarn to the front of the work, insert hook from front to back in BL of first dc from the end of the last petal (3rd st up from base of petal), make the next sc, pulling the last yo through all lps on hook, hdc 1 in the same st), (3 hdc) in next ch, (hdc, 2 dc) in next ch, dc, htr, tr. Sk 3 sts of rnd 4, sl st in next st.

Petal 12: Work same as petal 17, stopping after the tr. Cut yarn, leaving a long tail for sewing. Pull yarn end up out of the last tr, in preparation for a needle join. Needle join around the very first sl st of the petal rnd. Weave tail up the back of the petal to

FOR THESE FLOWERS WE USED

Lion Brand Sock-Ease™ (75% wool, 25% nylon; 3.5oz/100g = 438yd/400m): (A) and (B) color Lemon Drop #204—super fine weight yarn; (1)

GAUGE CIRCLE
(see page 11) = 1¹⁄₁₆"/1.7cm worked on 3.25mm (size 0 steel U.S.) hook

FINISHED MEASUREMENTS
3⅜"/8.5cm

Brown Sheep Company Lamb's Pride (85% wool, 15% mohair; 4oz/113g = 190yd/173m): (A) color Orange You Glad #M110; (C) color Wild Mustard #M174—worsted weight yarn; (4)

GAUGE CIRCLE
(see page 11) = 1³⁄₁₆"/3cm worked on 5.00mm (size H-8 U.S.) hook

FINISHED MEASUREMENTS
6"/15.2cm

Lion Brand LB Collection Cotton Bamboo (52% cotton, 48% rayon from bamboo; 3.5oz/100g = 245yd/224m): (A) colors Gardenia #170 and Hyacinth #107, (B) color Persimmon #135—light weight yarn; (3)

GAUGE CIRCLE
(see page 11) = 1"/2.5cm worked on 4.00mm (size G-6 U.S.) hook.

FINISHED MEASUREMENTS
5"/12.7cm

the 3rd dc from the base. Stitch under the back of the 5th sc of first petal, pulling so that the curl of the first petal overlaps the curved edge of the last petal. Stitch back into the last petal.

Finishing

Weave in ends. Wet block or steam with absolutely no pressure from the iron. Smooth the petals' curves and tweak their curls. Let dry.

Perspective Daisy

We tend to crochet flowers as if we're looking at them straight on, but in nature we see flowers from many angles. This design acknowledges perspective. Make the daisy double, as written, or use single petal layers to embellish your projects.

INSTRUCTIONS

Upper Petal Layer

With A, ch 5, join with sl st in first ch to form a ring.

Rnd 1: Ch 1, sc in ring, (make a 4-st petal, sc in ring) 3 times; make a 5-st petal, sc in ring; make a 7-st petal, sc in ring; (make an 8-st petal, sc in ring) twice; make a 7-st petal, sc in ring; make a 5-st petal, cut yarn and needle join in first sc of rnd.

Lower Petal Layer

With A, ch 5, join with sl st in first ch to form a ring.

Rnd 1: Ch 1, sc in ring, (make a 4-st petal, sc in ring) twice; make a 5-st petal, sc in ring; make a 6-st petal, sc in ring; make a 7-st petal, sc in ring; make an 8-st petal, sc in ring; make a 7-st petal, sc in ring; make a 6-st petal, sc in ring; make a 5-st petal, cut yarn and needle join to first sc of rnd.

Perspective Daisy

SKILL LEVEL
Easy

MATERIALS & TOOLS
2 colors of yarn of similar weight: petal color (A), center color (B)

Hook: Appropriate size hook to achieve a firm gauge with selected yarn

Tapestry needle

SPECIAL ABBREVIATIONS
Htr (half treble crochet): Yo 2 times, insert hook in stitch and draw up a loop (4 loops on hook), yo and draw through 2 loops (3 loops on hook), yo and draw through 3 loops (1 loop left on hook).

4-st petal: Ch 7, sc in 4th ch from hook, working back along chain, 2 hdc, sc.

5-st petal: Ch 8, sc in 4th ch from hook, working back along chain, 3 hdc, sc.

6-st petal: Ch 9, sc in 4th ch from hook, working back along chain, hdc, 2 dc, hdc, sc.

7-st petal: Ch 10, sc in 4th ch from hook, working back along chain, hdc, 3 dc, hdc, sc.

8-st petal: Ch 11, sc in 4th ch from hook, working back along chain, hdc, dc, 2 htr, dc, hdc, sc.

Blue Sky Alpacas Alpaca Silk (50% alpaca, 50% silk; 1.75oz/50g = 146yd/133m): (A) color Mango #144, (B) color Brick #126—fine weight yarn; (**2**)

GAUGE CIRCLE
(see page 11) = ¾"/1.9cm worked on 3.50mm (size E-4 U.S.) hook

FINISHED MEASUREMENTS
2⅞"/7.3cm for Perspective Daisy; 2½"/6cm for Straight-on Daisy with 5-st petals; 3⅛"/7.9cm for Straight-on Daisy with 7-st petals.

Lion Brand Lion® Cotton (100% cotton; 5oz/142g = 236yd/215m (solid colors)): (A) color White #100; (B) color Sunflower #157—medium weight yarn; (**4**)

GAUGE CIRCLE
(see page 11) = 1⁵⁄₁₆"/3.3cm worked on 5.00mm (size H-8 U.S.) hook

FINISHED MEASUREMENTS
4¼"/10.8cm for Perspective Daisy; 4⅜"/11.1cm for Straight-on Daisy with 6-st petals.

Straight-on
Daisy Variation

Center

With B, ch 4, join with sl st in first ch to form a ring.

Rnd 1: Ch 1, 8 sc in ring, cut yarn, leaving a long tail for sewing, and needle join to first st of rnd.

Straight-on Daisy Variation, both layers

With A, ch 5, join with sl st in first ch to form a ring.

Rnd 1: Ch 1, sc in ring, (make the petal-size of your choice, sc in ring) 8 times; make one more petal in the same size, cut yarn and needle join to first sc of rnd.

Make a Center as described above.

Finishing

Place the Upper Petal Layer on the Lower Petal Layer, with the centers and petal sizes matching. Adjust so that the petals of the Lower Petal Layer peek out from between the top petals. Pin or tack if desired. Place Center over the original center ring of the petal layers and sew in place taking the thread through the center and just inside the top of every other of the Center's sc. If desired use A, B, or C to sew petal layers together with one long stitch to every petal on the Upper Petal Layer, running from the base of the petal to 2 or 3 sts up the petal and just catching the edge stitch of the corresponding petal on the Lower Petal Layer.

Van Wyk Rose

Painter and author Helen Van Wyk urged her students to look for the basic shapes in flowers. Her basic rose shape is perfect for crochet.

SKILL LEVEL
Beginner

MATERIALS & TOOLS
1-4 colors of yarn of similar weight: petal color (A), additional, optional petal colors (B and C), greenery color (D)

Hook: Appropriate size hook to achieve a firm gauge with selected yarn

Tapestry needle

PATTERN NOTE
For color variation, make each part of the flower in different values of the same color, going from light to dark or vice versa.

INSTRUCTIONS

Center

With A, leaving a long tail for sewing, ch 4, join with sl st in first ch to form a ring.

Rnd 1: Ch 1, 8 sc in ring, join with sl st to first st of rnd—8 sc.

Rnd 2: Ch 1, *(2 sc) in next st, sc; rep from * 3 times, join with sl st to first st of rnd—12 sc.

Rnd 3: Ch 1, sc in each st around, join with sl st to first st of rnd.

Rnd 4: Ch 1, *sc, sc2tog; rep from * 3 times, cut yarn and needle join to first st of rnd—8 sc.

Second Petal Set

With B or desired color, leaving a long tail for sewing, ch 5, join with sl st in first ch to form a ring.

Rnd 1: Ch 2 (counts as hdc), 11 hdc in ring, join with sl st to top of ch-2 at beg of rnd—12 hdc.

Rnd 2: Ch 2, hdc in same st as sl st join, [(2 hdc) in next st] 11 times, join with sl st to top of ch-2 at beg of rnd—24 hdc.

Rnd 3: Ch 2, hdc in each st around, join with sl st to top of ch-2 at beg of rnd.

Rnd 4: Ch 1, sc in each st around, cut yarn and needle join to first st of rnd—24 sc.

FOR THESE FLOWERS WE USED

Berroco Ultra® Alpaca (50% super fine alpaca, 50% Peruvian wool; 3.5oz/100g = 215yd/198m): (A, B, and C) various combinations of colors red #6234, yellow #6225, orange #6263, dark red #6236; (D) color green #6262—light weight yarn; (3)

GAUGE CIRCLE
(see page 11) = 1"/2.5cm worked on 4.00mm (size G-6 U.S.) hook

FINISHED MEASUREMENTS
2⅜"/6cm without leaf

Prism Symphony (80% merino, 10% cashmere, 10% nylon; 2oz/56g = 118yd/107m): (A, B, and C) color Sunrise or Lipstick, (D) color Moss—medium weight yarn; (4)

GAUGE CIRCLE
(see page 11) = 1"/2.5cm worked on 4.00mm (size G-6 U.S.) hook

FINISHED MEASUREMENTS
2¼"/5.7cm without leaf

Third Petal Set

With C or desired color, ch 5, join with sl st in first ch to form a ring.

Rnd 1: Ch 3 (counts as one dc), 15 dc in ring, join with sl st to top of ch-3 at beg of rnd—16 dc.

Rnd 2: Ch 3, dc in same st as sl st join, (2 dc in next st) 15 times, join with sl st to top of ch-3 at beg of rnd—32 dc.

Rnd 3: Ch 3, dc in each st around, join with sl st to top of ch-3 at beg of rnd.

Rnd 4: Ch 1, sc in each st around, cut yarn and needle join to first st of rnd—32 sc.

Leaf (optional)

With D, make the first 2 rnds of the Coleus leaf (page 34).

Finishing

Weave in ends except for long tails for sewing. Place Center into Second Petal Set, and sew together with tail from Center piece. Place Second Petal Set into Third Petal Set. Sew them together with a few stitches, using the tail. If desired, tack a leaf so it peeks out from under the Van Wyk Rose.

Samarkand Sunflower

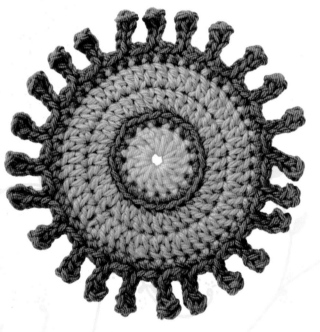

Small Samarkand Sunflower

The people of the ancient city of Samarkand produced beautiful pottery and textiles. This flower is based on a similar flower—or maybe a sun in a Samarkand weaving. The original colors are red, gold, and cream on a green background.

Large Samarkand Sunflower

INSTRUCTIONS

Large Flower

Ch 5, join with sl st in first ch to form a ring.

Rnd 1: With A, ch 3 (counts as 1 dc), 15 dc in ring, needle join or join with sl st to top of ch-3 at beg of rnd and fasten off—16 dc.

Rnd 2: Join B with sc in any st of rnd 1, 2 sc in next st, *sc, (2 sc) in next st; rep from * 6 more times, needle join or join with sl st in first st of rnd and fasten off—24 sc.

Rnd 3: Join C with dc in BL of any st of rnd 2. Working the rest of the rnd in BL only, (2 dc) in next st, *dc, (2 dc) in next st; rep from * 10 more times, join with sl st in first st of rnd—36 dc.

Rnd 4: Continuing with the same color, ch 3, dc in same st as join of previous rnd, 2 dc, *(2 dc) in next st, dc in each of next 2 sts; rep from * 10 more times. Needle join

SKILL LEVEL
Easy

MATERIALS & TOOLS
3 colors of yarn of similar weight: yellow or center color (A), off-white or center outline and petal color (B), and red or middle section color (C)

Hook: Appropriate size hook to achieve a firm gauge with selected yarn

Tapestry needle

PATTERN NOTE
For finest results, needle join every time you fasten off.

FOR THESE FLOWERS WE USED

Earth Arts's Naturally Dyed Navajo-Churro Yarn (100% wool, 4oz/113g = approximately 175yd/159m): (A) color golden yellow, (B) color off-white, (C) color burgundy—bulky weight yarn; (5)

After finishing, the flowers were felted in the washing machine.

GAUGE CIRCLE
(see page 11) = 1¼/3.1cm worked on 5.00mm (size H-8 U.S.) hook

FINISHED MEASUREMENTS
6 3/4"/17.1cm (large); 5¾/14.6cm (medium); 4¼"/10.8cm (small)

Spud and Chloë Sweater (55% superwash wool, 45% organic cotton; 3.5oz/100g = 160yd/146m): (A) color Firefly #7505, (B) color Jelly Bean #7513, (C) color Watermelon #7512—medium weight yarn; (4)

GAUGE CIRCLE
(see page 11) = 1¼"/3cm worked on 5.00mm (size H-8 U.S.) hook

FINISHED MEASUREMENTS
6"/15.3cm (large); 5⅛"/13cm (medium); 3⅝"/9.2cm (small)

to first st of rnd or join with sl st to first st of rnd and fasten off—48 dc.

Rnd 5: Join B with sc in any st of rnd 4, ch 5, hdc in 2nd ch from hook, sl st in next 3 ch, sc in next st of rnd 4, *sc in next st of rnd 4, ch 5, hdc in 2nd ch from hook, sl st in next 3 ch, sc in next st of rnd 4; rep from * around. Needle join to first st of rnd—24 petals.

Medium Flower
Work rnds 1-3 as for Large Flower, except needle join and fasten off at the end of rnd 3.

Rnd 4: Join B with sc in any st of rnd 3, ch 5, hdc in 2nd ch from hook, sl st in next 3 ch, sc in next st of rnd 3, *sc in next st of rnd 3, ch 5, hdc in 2nd ch from hook, sl st in next 3 ch, sc in next st of rnd 3; rep from * around. Needle join to first st of rnd—18 petals.

Small Flower
Work rnds 1-2 as for Large Flower.

Rnd 3: Join C with sc in BL of any st of rnd 2. Ch 4, hdc in 2nd ch from hook, sl st in each of next 2 ch, sc in BL of next st of rnd 2. Making all the rem sc of this rnd in BL only of rnd 2, *sc in next st of rnd 2, ch 4, hdc in 2nd ch from hook, sl st in each of next 2 ch, sc in next st of rnd 2; rep from * around. Needle join over first st of rnd.

Finishing
Weave in ends. If desired, felt the flowers that are made from non-superwash wool. Otherwise, block.

Medium
Samarkand
Sunflowers

Curlicue Sprays

You'll find curlicues and sprays paired with flowers in many decorative arts. They add a finishing flourish to a flower, and they also look good on their own.

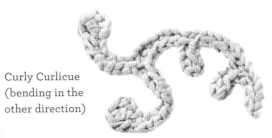

Curly Curlicue (bending in the other direction)

Little Flower

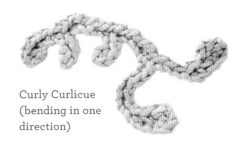

Curly Curlicue (bending in one direction)

INSTRUCTIONS

Leafy Curlicue Spray

(Ch 9, sl st in 3rd ch from hook, sc, (hdc, dc) in next ch, dc, hdc-sc-tog, sl st, ch 5 for center stem) twice.

FIRST CURLICUE

Ch 12, hdc in 3rd ch from hook, ch 2, sc in the ch beyond the hdc, (2 sl st) in each of the next 3 ch, 5 sl sts.

TOP LEAF

Ch 1, reach backwards with the hook and sl st in next to last sl st of First curlicue, ch 10, sl st in 3rd ch from hook, sc, hdc, 2 dc, hdc, sc, 3 sl sts.

SECOND CURLICUE

Ch 1, reach backwards with the hook and sl st in next to last sl st of Top leaf, ch 14, dc in 4th ch from hook, sc2tog, (sk 1 ch, sl st) 3 times, 4 sl sts, draw up a lp in st at base of Top leaf, draw up a lp in next ch st of stem (3 lps on hook), yo, draw through all lps on hook, sc, 3 sl sts in ch of center stem.

Now you're opposite of a leaf: *Ch 9, sl st in 3rd ch from hook, sc, hdc-dc-tog, dc, (hdc, sc) in next st, sl st. *

5 sl sts along ch of center stem, rep bet * and *.

For stem, ch 9 or desired length, hdc in 2nd ch from hook, sl st in each rem ch, cut yarn and needle join in first st at the bottom of the first leaf.

Curly Curlicue (bending in one direction)

Ch 4 for stem.

SMALL CURVES

*Ch 5, (2 sl sts) in 4th ch from hook, sl st, ch 4 for stem; rep from * once.

SKILL LEVEL
Intermediate

MATERIALS & TOOLS
One or two colors of yarn in similar weights: curlicue color (A), flower color (B)

Hook: Appropriate size hook to achieve a firm gauge with selected yarn

Tapestry needle

SPECIAL ABBREVIATIONS
Hdc-sc-tog: Yo, insert hook in next stitch, yo and draw up a loop, insert hook in next st, yo and draw up a loop (4 loops on hook), yo and draw through remaining loops on hook.

Hdc-dc-tog: Yo, insert hook in next stitch, yo and draw up a loop, yo, insert hook in next st, yo and draw up a loop (5 loops on hook), yo, draw through 2 loops on hook, yo, draw through remaining loops on hook.

BIG CURLICUE

Ch 16, dc in 4th ch from hook, sc2tog, (sk 1 ch, sl st) 4 times, sl st, (2 sl sts) in next st.

SMALL CURLICUE

Ch 12, dc in 4th ch from hook, sc2tog, (sk 1 ch, sl st) 2 times, 2 sl sts.

Sc in first ch st of stem, (2 sl sts) in each of next 3 ch, *ch 1, sk over the base of the Small Curve and (2 sl sts) in each of the next 4 ch; rep from * once. Fasten off.

Curly Curlicue (bending in the other direction)
Ch 23 for stem.

FOR THESE FLOWERS WE USED
Prism Angora (100% French angora; 1oz/28g = 90yd/82m): (A) color Peacock—light weight yarn; (**3**)

GAUGE CIRCLE
(see page 11) = 15⁄16"/2.4cm worked on 4.00mm (size G-6 U.S.) hook

FINISHED MEASUREMENTS
3"/7.6cm x 5¼"/13.3cm (leafy spray); 3¼"/8.2cm x 2"/5.1cm (curly curlicue)

SMALL CURLICUE

Ch 9, dc in 4th ch from hook, ch 2, sc in next ch, (sl st 2) in each of the next 2 sts, 2 sl sts.

BIG CURLICUE

Ch 12, dc in 4th ch from hook, ch 2, sc in next ch, (sl st 2) in each of the next 4 sts, sl st, sk 1 ch, sl st.

Stem and small curves
Sc in first ch st of stem, (sk 1 ch, sl st) 3 times *ch 6, sl st in 3rd ch from hook, sk 1 st, sl st, (sk 1 ch of stem, sl st) 4 times; rep from * once. Fasten off.

Little Flower
Ch 3, join with sl st in first ch to form a ring.

Rnd 1: Ch 1, *sc in ring, ch 6, dc in 4th ch from hook, hdc, sc; rep from * 4 times, cut yarn and needle join to first st of rnd.

Finishing
Weave in ends. Pull, stretch, and shape curves before blocking. Block.

Berroco Suede® (100% nylon; 1.75oz/50g = 120yd/111m): (A) color Dale Evans #3727, (B) color Campfire #3739—medium weight yarn; (**4**)

GAUGE CIRCLE
(see page 11) = 1"/2.5cm worked on 4.00mm (size G-6 U.S.) hook

FINISHED MEASUREMENTS
3⅛"/7.9cm x 5⅜"/13.7cm (leafy spray); 3⅜"/8.5cm x 2³⁄16"/5.5cm (curly curlicue); 2⅛"/5.4cm (little flower)

Leafy Curlicue Sprays

Tabby Oval

Inspired by ethnic Hungarian embroidery, this appealing flower surprises and delights with its funny shape and its many color possibilities. Practice your needle-joining skills so your flower will look as seamless as possible.

SKILL LEVEL
Intermediate

MATERIALS & TOOLS
Up to 6 colors of yarn of similar weight: center colors (A, B, and C), petal colors (D, E, and F)

Hook: Appropriate size hook to achieve a firm gauge with selected yarn

Tapestry needle

SPECIAL ABBREVIATIONS
BPdc (Back Post double crochet): Yo, insert hook from back to front between the st you just finished and the next stitch. Push hook to the back between the next stitch and the stitch after that. At this point, you'll see your hook across the front of the next stitch, and the top of the stitch that you would normally crochet in (but not this time), is pushed toward you. Yo, draw up a loop that will come around the front of the stitch, (yo, draw through 2 loops) twice.

BPdc-hdc inc (Back Post double crochet-half double crochet increase): Work a BPdc as described above. Yo and insert hook in the base of the BPdc at the back of the work. It looks like two sideways strands around the st below. Yo and draw up a loop, yo and draw through all 3 loops on hook.

BPsc (Back Post single crochet): Yo, insert hook from back to front between the stitch you just finished and the next stitch. Push hook to the back between the next stitch and the stitch after that. Yo, draw up a loop that will come around the front of the st, yo, draw through both loops.

PATTERN NOTE
The pattern is written for 6 colors, but you can change colors or not as desired. However even if you only use one color for the center of the Tabby Oval, I recommend cutting the yarn and needle joining after rounds 2, 3, and 4 for the best finished appearance. If it helps, read "Do What It Takes" in the Basics section (page 18).

INSTRUCTIONS

Flower Center

Rnd 1: With A, ch 9, sc in 4th ch from hook, 5 sc, ch 3, sl st in free lp at base of the last sc.

Rnd 2: Ch 3, dc in same st as sl st, working in free lps of ch along the base of previous rnd, 4 dc, (2 dc) in next st, (6 dc) in ch-3 sp. Rotate the piece so you are looking at the tops of the sc of previous rnd, (2 dc) in next sc, 4 dc, (2 dc) in last sc, (6 dc) in ch-3 sp, cut yarn and needle join to top of ch-3 at beg of rnd—28 dc.

Rnd 3: Join B with BPdc around ch-3 at beg of last rnd, 7 BPdc, 7 BPdc-hdc inc, 6 BPdc, 7 BPdc-hdc inc, cut yarn and needle join to first st of rnd—42 sts.

FOR THESE FLOWERS WE USED

Berroco Ultra® Alpaca (50% super fine alpaca, 50% Peruvian wool; 3.5oz/100g = 215yd/198m): (A) color heathery purple #62171 (B) color teal #6285; (C) color heathery red violet 6259; (D) color orange #6263; (E) color red #6234; (F) color brick red #6236—light weight yarn; (3)

GAUGE CIRCLE
(see page 11) = 1"/2.5cm worked on 4.00mm (size G-6 U.S.) hook

FINISHED MEASUREMENTS
7"/17.8cm x 6"/15.2cm

Blue Sky Alpacas Worsted Cotton (100% organic cotton; 3.5oz/100g = 150yd/137m): (A and C) color Sand #81; (B and D) color Bone #80; (E) color Ladybug #629; (F) color Caribbean # 630—medium weight yarn; (4)

GAUGE CIRCLE
(see page 11) = 1⅜"/3.5cm worked on 5.50mm (size I-9 U.S) hook

FINISHED MEASUREMENTS
9.5"/24.1cm x 8"/20.3cm

Rnd 4: Join C with BPdc around first st of last rnd, 7 BPdc, (BPdc-hdc inc, BPdc) 7 times, 7 BPdc, (BPdc-hdc inc, BPdc) 6 times, BPdc-hdc inc, cut yarn and needle join to first st of rnd—56 sts.

Rnd 5: Rejoin C with a BPsc around first st of last rnd, 3 BPsc, PM in st you just finished, then BPsc in each rem st around, cut yarn and needle join to first st of rnd—56 sts.

Flower Petals

Rnd 6: Join D with sl st in marked st of rnd 5, remove marker. *Ch 8, hdc in 4th ch from hook, 4 hdc, sk 1 st of the rnd below, sl st in next st, ch 5, sk 5 sts of the rnd

below, sl st in next st; rep from * 5 times. Rep from * once more, except after you sk 5 sts of the rnd below, do not sl st in the next st. Instead, cut yarn and needle join to first st of rnd—7 petals comprised of 5 hdc with a ch-3 sp at the top.

Rnd 7: Keep the ch-5 lps of the previous row out of the way to the WS. Count back 2 sts from beg of rnd 6 and join E with sl st. *In free lps of the ch going up the side of the next petal, hdc2tog, 3 hdc, (7 hdc) in ch-3 lp at top of petal, (2 hdc) in next hdc, 4 hdc, sk 1 st of rnd 5, sl st in next st, ch 1, sk 1 st of rnd 5, ‡ sl st in next st; rep from * 5 times. Rep bet * and ‡ once, cut yarn and needle join to first st of rnd.

Rnd 8: Find the sc of rnd 5 between any 2 petals and join F with *sl st in the sc (of rnd 5), catching the ch-5 of rnd 6 and the ch-1 from rnd 7 in the sl st, sc in first st of next petal, hdc2tog, hdc, (2 hdc in next st, 1 hdc in next st) 4 times, (2 hdc) in next st, 3 hdc, sc; rep from * 6 times, cut yarn and needle join to first st of rnd.

Finishing

Weave in ends. Block gently, being careful not to squash the ribs in the center of the flower. Add embellishments to center of flower as desired.

Byzantine Beauty

Ancient Byzantium lent its name to anything needlessly complicated. Based on a Byzantine-style boss or circular ornament, this flower is exactly complicated enough. It becomes easier to make with practice.

INSTRUCTIONS

Petal Round 1

With waste yarn, ch 24, join with sl st in first ch to form a ring. Fasten off.

Rnd 1: With A, ch 2, *2 sl sts in waste yarn ring, ch 25, sk 6 sts of waste yarn ring; rep from * once, 2 sl sts in waste yarn ring, ch 23, join with sl st in first ch st of rnd.

Rnd 2: Ch 1, working in each ch, beg with the one with the sl st, 16 sc, *(sc, ch 2, sc) in next ch, 26 sc; rep from * once, (sc, ch 2, sc) in next ch, 10 sc, join with sl st to first st of rnd or needle-join. Fasten off.

Rnd 3: Beg in first st of rnd 2, join B with *6 sc, (sc2tog) twice, (sc, 2 sc in next st) 2 times, 3 sc, (hdc, sl st-picot, hdc) in the ch-2 sp, 3 sc, (2 sc in next st, sc) 2 times,

(sc2tog) twice; rep from * twice, join with sl st to first st of rnd or needle-join. Fasten off.

Petal Round 2

With A, ch 82.

Row 1: Beg in 2nd ch from hook, 16 sc, *(sc, ch 2, sc) in next ch, 26 sc; rep from * once, (sc, ch 2, sc) in next ch, 10 sc. Fasten off. Do not turn.

Row 2: Beg at the ch-1 end of row 1 (yarn ends will be on the other end). With B, *6 sc, (sc2tog) twice, (sc, 2 sc in next st) 2 times, 3 sc, (hdc, sl st-picot, hdc) in the ch-2 sp, 3 sc, (2 sc in next st, sc) 2 times, (sc2tog) twice; rep from * twice. Fasten off.

Inner Ring

With C, ch 37.

Row 1: Beg in 2nd ch from hook, 3 sc, *(2 sc in next st), 5 sc; rep from * 4 times, (2 sc in next st), 2 sc. Fasten off—42 sc.

If you want to use an eyelash yarn for this rnd as in the photo, make the ch with A or B, then work row 1 with the eyelash yarn. Use the best-looking side as the RS when you weave—usually it's the back side of the sc.

Outer Ring (optional)

With D or desired color, ch 43.

Row 1: Beg in 2nd ch from hook, 4 sc, *(2 sc in next st), 6 sc; rep from * 4 times, (2 sc in next st), 2 sc. Fasten off—48 sc.

SKILL LEVEL
Experienced

MATERIALS & TOOLS
4 or 5 colors of yarn of similar weight: petal colors (A and B), one or two ring colors (C and D), optional greenery color (E)

Hook: Appropriate size hook to achieve a firm gauge with selected yarn

Waste yarn, Tapestry needle

SPECIAL ABBREVIATION
Sl st-picot: Ch 3, sl st in base of chain.

PATTERN NOTE
Chain a few extra stitches for the second petal round to avoid running out of stitches. Pick out the leftovers. Read "Doing What it Takes," page 18, if you need moral support.

FOR THESE FLOWERS WE USED

Caron International Naturally Caron Country (25% merino wool, 75% microdenier acrylic; 3oz/85g = 185yd/170m): (A, B, C, and D) in various combinations as in photo: colors Spice House #0018, Gilder Age #0011, Soft Sunshine #0003, Naturally #0007, Claret #0017; (E) color Loden Forest #0020--medium weight yarn; (4)

For one flower, (C) Lion Brand Festive Fur (80% polyester, 20% metallic polyester; 1.75oz/50g = 55yd/50m): color Gold #170--bulky weight yarn; (5)

GAUGE CIRCLE
(see page 11) = 1"/2.5cm worked on 4.00mm (size G-6 U.S.) hook

FINISHED MEASUREMENTS
6⅛"/15.5cm

Leaves (optional)
Make one or two Ladder Leaf motifs (page 71) without stems.

Finishing
Block the pieces gently to flatten them out a little. Lay out petal round 1 in a roughly triangular shape with the points where the points of the triangle would be; the waste yarn row will pull in the sides. *Weave petal round 2 under one side of a petal and over the other side of the petal; rep from * twice. Adjust it so the petal tops are between the petal tops of petal round 1, and the join of petal round 1 is behind petal round 2. Sew the ends of petal round 1 together—I prefer to needle

join the 2nd row and use the other ends to sew the rest.

Note where the petal edges cross: Outside of where they cross, weave the Inner Ring over and under the edges of the petals. Sew its ends tog and adjust the Inner Ring so that its join will be under a petal edge.

If desired, weave Outer Ring under and over the petal edges, opposite of Inner Ring. Sew ends together and hide join behind a petal.

Unravel and remove waste yarn. Pull petals, scrunch and stretch flower to settle it in its correct position. Refer to photo to

help you decide when it is right. Weave in ends and block again, first from the back, and then again from the front.

If desired, sew the Ladder Leaf (page 71) behind petals as shown in photo.

Tole Tulip

Tole painting and traditional embroideries inspired the curvy petals of this tulip. Crocheted in green, this versatile piece makes a nice leaf, too. It looks good from either side.

SKILL LEVEL
Intermediate

MATERIALS & TOOLS
2 colors of yarn of similar weight: flower color (A), leaf color (B)

Hook: Appropriate size hook to achieve a firm gauge with selected yarn

Tapestry needle

SPECIAL ABBREVIATION
Htr (half treble crochet): Yo 2 times, insert hook into stitch and draw up a loop (4 loops on hook), yo and draw through 2 loops (3 loops on hook), yo and draw through 3 loops (1 loop left on hook).

FOR THESE FLOWERS WE USED

Berroco Ultra® Alpaca (50% super fine alpaca, 50% Peruvian wool; 3.5oz/100g = 215yd/198m): (A) color red #6234 or burgundy #6281; (B) color green #6273—light weight yarn; (**3**)

GAUGE CIRCLE
(see page 11) = 1"/2.5cm worked on 4.00mm (size G-6 U.S.) hook

FINISHED MEASUREMENTS
2¾"/7cm x 3½"/9cm (2 picots each side); 2"/5.1cm x 2¾"/7cm (1 picot each side); 4⅛"/10.4cm x 4½"/11.4cm (4 picots each side)

Lion Brand Lion® Cotton (100% cotton; 5oz/142g = 236yd/215m (solid colors)): (A) color Sunflower #157 or Poppy Red #112—medium weight yarn; (**4**)

GAUGE CIRCLE
(see page 11) = 1⁵⁄₁₆"/3.3cm worked on 5.00mm (size H-8 U.S.) hook

FINISHED MEASUREMENTS
3⅝"/9.2cm x 4⅜"/11.1cm (2 picots each side); 4½"/11.4cm x 5⅛"/13cm (3 picots each side)

Louet Euroflax Sport (100% wet spun linen; 3.5oz/100g = 270yd/246m): (A) color Pink Panther #51; (B) color Shamrock #17—light weight yarn; (**2**)

GAUGE CIRCLE
(see page 11) = ¾"/2cm worked on 3.50mm (size E-4 U.S.) hook

FINISHED MEASUREMENTS
2¾"/7cm x 3¼"/8.2cm (2 picot each side); 2"/5.1cm x 2⅝"/6.6cm (1 picot each side)

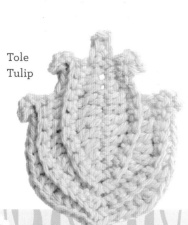

Tole Tulip

Tole Tulip Variation

Tole Tulip Variation with Rows Repeated Twice

Tole Tulip

Tole Tulip
with Sepal
and Stem

Leaf

INSTRUCTIONS

Flower

Row 1 (RS): Ch 15, sc in 4th ch from hook, 3 sc, hdc, 2 dc, 2 htr, dc, hdc, sc, ch 2. Rotate the piece so you can work in the free lps on the other side of the ch. Sc, hdc, dc, 2 htr, 2 dc, hdc, 2 sc. Some sts rem unworked. Ch 4, draw up a lp in 2nd ch, 3rd ch, and 4th ch from hook (4 lps on hook). Yo, draw through all lps on hook. Turn—22 sts, ch-2 sp, 1 curvy picot.

Row 2: Working in BL only, 10 sc, (sc, ch 2, sc) in ch-2 sp. Rotate the piece so you can work along the other side, 10 sc. Some sts rem unworked. Ch 4, draw up a lp in 2nd ch, 3rd ch, and 4th ch from hook (4 lps on hook). Yo, draw through all lps on hook. Turn—22 sc, ch-2 sp, 1 curvy picot.

Row 3: Working in BL only, 4 sc, hdc, 2 dc, (2 htr) in next st, dc, hdc, sc, (sc, ch 2, sc) in ch-2 sp, sc, hdc, dc, (2 htr) in next st, 2 dc, hdc, sc. Some sts rem unworked. Ch 4, draw up a lp in 2nd ch, 3rd ch, and 4th ch from hook (4 lps on hook). Yo, draw through all lps on hook. Turn—23 sts, ch-2 sp, 1 curvy picot.

Row 4: Rep row 2.

Row 5: Working in BL only, 4 sc, hdc, 2 dc, (2 htr) in next st, dc, hdc, sc, (sc, ch 2, sc) in ch-2 sp, sc, hdc, dc, (2 htr) in next st, 2 dc, hdc, 3 sc, needle join to next st, which is just under the picot.

Variation

Rep rows 2 and 3 once more or as desired before going on to rows 4 and 5.

Leaf

Work as for Flower, Rows 1–3.

Sepal and Stem

Row 1: With B, ch 4, (4 dc, ch 3, sl st) in 4th ch from hook, ch desired length of stem, adding leaves as desired with sl st in base of leaf.

Row 2: Sl st in 2nd ch from hook, sl st in rem sts, adding leaves as desired.

Finishing

Sew sepal to bottom edge of flower. Weave in ends.

Turkestani Star

Shaded motifs are common in textile works, like the Turkestani folk embroidery that inspired this flower. Dyeing shaded threads of the same hue is as simple as removing yarns from the dye bath at different times, so they have varying amounts of the dye in them.

SKILL LEVEL
Easy

MATERIALS & TOOLS
3 colors of yarn of similar weight, which are dark, medium, and light values of the same color (A, B, and C)

Hook: Appropriate size hook to achieve a firm gauge with selected yarn

Buttons or other flower centers as desired

Tapestry needle

PATTERN NOTE
Use colors in order from darkest to lightest or the other way around.

FOR THESE FLOWERS WE USED

Cascade 220 Wool (100% Peruvian Highland wool; 3.5oz/100g = 220yd/200m): (A) color pale pink #9477 or lavender #8912, (B) color pink #9478 or purple #7808, (C) color dark pink #2428 or dark purple #8886 (or the same colors, except going from dark to light)—medium weight yarn; (4) ; sparkly button by Gail Hughes

GAUGE CIRCLE
(see page 11) = 1"/2.5cm worked on 4.00mm (size G-6 U.S.) hook

FINISHED MEASUREMENTS
4¼"/10.8cm

Coats & Clark's Aunt Lydia's Classic Crochet Thread, No. 10, Art. 154 (100% Mercerized Cotton, 350yd/320m): (A) color Cream #420, (B) color Golden Yellow #422, (C) color Goldenrod #421 (or the same colors, except going from dark to light)—10-count crochet thread; (0)

GAUGE CIRCLE
(see page 11) = ⅜"/0.9cm worked on 2.00mm (size 4 steel U.S.) hook

FINISHED MEASUREMENTS
2"/5cm

INSTRUCTIONS

Flower

With A, ch 4, join with sl st in first ch to form a ring.

Rnd 1: Ch 1, *sc in ring, ch 9, sc in 4th ch from hook, 5 sc; rep from * 4 times, cut yarn and needle join to first sc of rnd.

Rnd 2: Counting from center, find the 2nd sc of a petal. Join B with sc in ch at the base of this sc. 4 sc, (4 sc) in ch-sp at tip of petal, 5 sc. Draw up a lp in next st, sk 1 sc, draw up a lp in base of next sc, yo, draw through all 3 lps on hook (petal dec made). *5 sc, (4 sc) in ch-sp at tip of petal,

5 sc, make a petal dec as above; rep from * 3 times, cut yarn and needle join to first sc of rnd.

Rnd 3: Find the petal dec st, sk 2 sts, and join C with sc in the next st, 2 sc, (2 sc) in each of the next 4 sts, 4 sc, Draw up a lp in next st, sk 2 sts, draw up a lp in next st, yo, draw through all lps on hook (longer petal dec made). *3 sc, (2 sc) in each of the next 4 sts, 4 sc, make a longer petal dec as above; rep from * 3 times, cut yarn and needle join to first sc of rnd.

Variation

When you have made this flower and understand the decreases between petals and the increases over the end of each petal, you can lengthen or shorten (a little) the petals as desired.

Finishing

Weave in ends. Add a flower center if desired.

Ladder Leaf

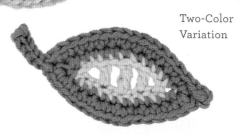

One-Color Leaf

Two-Color Variation

Embroiderers have come up with many ways to depict leaves and flowers. The Ladder Leaf is a testament to their expertise at distilling a shape to its essence. The natural torque of sc-in-the-round gives this leaf a graceful shape.

SKILL LEVEL
Easy

MATERIALS & TOOLS
1-3 colors of yarn of similar weight: leaf colors (A, B, and C)

Hook: Appropriate size hook to achieve a firm gauge with selected yarn

Tapestry needle

SPECIAL ABBREVIATION
Sl st-picot: Ch 3, sl st in base of chain.

FOR THESE LEAVES WE USED

Lion Brand LB Collection Cotton Bamboo (52% cotton, 48% rayon from bamboo; 3.5oz/100g = 245yd/224m): (A) color Gardenia #170; (B) color Snapdragon #174—light weight yarn; (3)

GAUGE CIRCLE
(see page 11) = 1"/2.5cm worked on 4.00mm (size G-6 U.S.) hook

FINISHED MEASUREMENTS
1⁷⁄₁₆"/4cm x 3⅜"/8.5cm (including stem)

Brooks Farm Yarns Duet (55% kid mohair, 45% fine wool; 8oz/225g = 500yd/455m): (A) color shaded greens/blues—light weight yarn; (3)

GAUGE CIRCLE
(see page 11) = ⅞"/2.2cm worked on 4.00mm (size G-6 U.S.) hook

FINISHED MEASUREMENTS
1¹¹⁄₁₆"/4.3cm x 3⅜"/8.1cm (including stem)

INSTRUCTIONS

One-Color Leaf

Rnd 1: Ch 13, dc in 6th ch from hook, ch 1, sk 1 st, tr, ch 1, sk 1, dc, ch 2.

Rnd 2: Join to first st of rnd 1 with sl st, ch 3, sc in same st as sl st. Working in BL of this rnd only, 9 sc, (sc, ch 2, sc) in next ch (which is the 3rd st of the turning ch), 10 sc, sl st in ch-3 sp at beg of rnd.

Rnd 3: Ch 3, sc in ch-3 sp at end of last rnd, 4 sc, (2 sc) in next st, sc, (2 sc) in next st, 4 sc, (hdc, sl st-picot, hdc) in ch-2 sp, 4 sc, (2 sc) in next st, sc, (2 sc) in next st, 4 sc, sc in ch-sp at end of last rnd, sl st in ch-3 lp.

If you don't want a stem, fasten off. If you want a stem, ch 6, sc in 2nd ch from hook, sl st in rem ch, cut thread and needle join in ch-2 sp.

Two-Color Variation

Rnd 1: With A, ch 13, dc in 6th ch from hook, ch 1, sk 1 st, tr, ch 1, sk 1, dc, ch 3, fasten off.

Rnd 2: Insert hook in first and last ch of rnd 1, with B, yo and pull a lp through both ch. Ch 3, sc in same sts. Working in BL of this rnd only, 9 sc, (sc, ch 2, sc) in next ch (which is the 3rd st of the turning ch), 9 sc, sc in joined ch from beg of rnd, sl st in ch-3 lp at beg of rnd.

Rnd 3: Continuing with B, Ch 3, sc in ch-3 sp at end of last rnd, 4 sc, (2 sc) in next st, sc, (2 sc) in next st, 4 sc, (hdc, sl st-picot, hdc) in ch-2 sp, 4 sc, (2 sc) in next st, sc, (2 sc) in next st, 4 sc, sc in ch-sp at end of last rnd, sl st in ch-3 lp. Make a stem as in One-color variation or fasten off.

Finishing

Weave in ends, block.

Burnished Placemats

The secret of stress-free crafting is to make each placemat and napkin a little different.

SKILL LEVEL
Easy

FINISHED MEASUREMENTS
Varies depending on size of placemats and napkins

MATERIALS & TOOLS
Coats & Clark Aunt Lydia's Classic Crochet Thread, No. 10, Art. 154, (100% mercerized cotton, 350yd/320m)—10-count crochet thread;

For all flower centers: color Goldenrod #0421

For the middle section of the medium and large flowers and petals of small flower: color Cream #0420

For the center outline of all flowers and petals of medium and large flowers: color Burgundy #0492

Crochet hook: 2.00mm (size 4 steel U.S.) or size to obtain gauge

Purchased placemats and napkins

Fabric glue

Small paintbrush for spreading glue

Sewing thread and needle

GAUGE CIRCLE
(see page 11) = ⅜"/0.9cm worked on 2.00mm (size 4 steel U.S.) hook

Instructions

For each placemat, crochet Samarkand Sunflowers (page 60): 1 large, 1 medium, 1 small.

Brush fabric glue onto the back of each flower, and press onto the placemat, using the photograph as a guide. Let dry.

Sew the end of each petal to the placemat. Sew around the inner outline of the flower.

For each napkin, crochet a medium Samarkand Sunflower. Glue and sew the flower to a corner of the napkin.

International Garden

Czech Festival Flowers

The women of the Czech Republic turn out for festivals in costumes covered in colorful embroidery, hand-made laces, and scalloped eyelet trims. In this wild exuberance, I once spotted these two demure little flowers on a sleeve panel, embroidered in red and outlined in black.

INSTRUCTIONS

Flower Within a Ring

With A, ch 5, join with sl st in first ch to form a ring.

Rnd 1: Ch 1, 12 sc in ring, join with sl st to first sc of rnd. Secure yarn but do not cut—12 sc.

Rnd 2: Join B in any st of rnd 1. *3 sc, (2 sc) in next st; rep from * 2 times, join with sl st to first sc of rnd. Secure yarn but do not cut—15 sc.

Rnd 3: Pick up A and *sl st, ch 3, 4-tr CL, placing the first tr in same st as sl st, 2nd and 3rd tr in next st, and 4th tr in next st, ch 3, sl st in same st as last tr; rep from * 4 times, join with sl st to first sc of rnd. Secure yarn but do not cut.

Rnd 4: Pick up B, yo. Find the nearest sp between petals. *Sc in the st of rnd 1 that is directly below the sp between petals—insert hook in a st that already has a B st from rnd 2. Sk 1 ch, working up the side of the petal, sc in each of the next 2 ch, 2 sc

across the top of the petal, sc in each of the next 2 ch, sk 1 ch; rep from * 4 times, join with sl st to first sc of rnd. Secure yarn but do not cut--sc outline for each petal, with a long sc between petals.

Rnd 5: Work in BL only for this rnd. Pick up A and find the top 2 sts of the nearest petal, *2 sl sts, sc, hdc, dc in long sc of the rnd below, hdc, sc; rep from * 4 times, join with sl st to first st of rnd. Fasten off A.

Rnd 6: Pick up B, yo, and beg in nearest dc of rnd 5, *2 sc, (2 sc) in next st, now you are at the top of a petal, where there are 2 sl sts from rnd 5. Sc in the st below each of the 2 sl sts. The sc will hide the sl sts. (2 sc) in next st, sc; rep from * 4 times, cut yarn and needle join to first st of rnd.

Flower Without a Ring

Work rnds 1-4 above, except end rnd 4 with a needle join.

SKILL LEVEL
Intermediate

MATERIALS & TOOLS
2 or more colors of yarn of similar weight: main color (A), outline color (B)

Hook: Appropriate size hook to achieve a firm gauge with selected yarn

Tapestry needle

SPECIAL ABBREVIATIONS
4 tr-CL: *Yo twice, insert hook in next stitch, yo and draw up a loop, (yo, draw through 2 loops on hook) twice; rep from * 3 times, yo, draw through all loops on hook, ch 1 to close the CL.

Sl st-picot: Ch 3, sl st in base of chain.

NOTE
To save weaving in many yarn ends, secure the yarn but do not cut. This means to open the last loop wide and pass the ball of yarn through the loop. Pull yarn to close loop.

The patterns are written for two colors. If you want to use multiple colors, I suggest keeping the outline rounds 2, 4, and 6 in one color, and vary the others.

Note that when you pick up a yarn that has been secured below, and the round begins with sc, I ask you to yo first. This lets you make a sc in the first st, with no need for the unsightly sl st-ch 1 that starts most sc rounds.

FOR THESE FLOWERS WE USED

Lion Brand LB Collection Superwash Merino (100% superwash merino wool; 3.5oz/100g = 306yd/280m): (A) color Antique #098, (B) color Sky #107—light weight yarn; (3)

GAUGE CIRCLE
(see page 11) = ⅞"/2.2cm worked on 4.00mm (size G-6 U.S.) hook.

FINISHED MEASUREMENTS
2½"/6.4cm (4 petal across widest point); 2⅝"/6.7cm (flower within a ring); 2"/5.1cm (flower without a ring); 1 ⅜"/3.5cm x 1¾"/4.4cm (leaf)

Cascade Yarns Jewel Hand Dyed (100% wool; 3.5oz/100g = 142yd/129m): (A) various colors Gold #9284, Blue #9282, Lavender #9281; (B) color Copper #9889—medium weight yarn; (4)

GAUGE CIRCLE
(see page 11) = 1⅜"/3.5cm worked on 6.00mm (size J-10 U.S.) hook

FINISHED MEASUREMENTS
3⅞"/9.9cm (4 petals across widest point); 4¼"/10.8cm (flower within a ring); 2⅛"/5.4cm x 2¾"/7cm (leaf)

Four Petal Flower

Flower Without a Ring

Four Petal Flower

With A, ch 5, join with sl st in first ch to form a ring.

Rnd 1: Ch 1, 12 sc in ring, join with sl st to first sc of rnd. Secure yarn but do not cut—12 sc.

Rnd 2: Join B in any st of rnd 1. *2 sc, (2 sc) in next st; rep from * 3 times, join with sl st to first sc of rnd. Secure yarn but do not cut—16 sc.

Rnd 3: Pick up A, yo, and in the closest st of rnd 3, *sc, ch 1, (dc, tr) in next st, tr, (tr, dc) in next st, ch 1; rep from * 3 times, join with sl st to first sc of rnd. Fasten off A.

Rnd 4: Pick up B, and in closest sc of rnd 3, *sl st, sk ch, (2 sc in next st) 5 times, sk ch; rep from * 3 times, cut yarn and needle join to first st of rnd.

Leaf

Rnd 1: With B, ch 6, sc in 3rd ch from hook, 3 sc. Secure yarn but do not cut.

Rnd 2: Rotate row 1 so you are looking at the original ch, which already has sts in it. Join A with sl st in free lp of the first ch. Ch 2, working along free lps of the original ch, (2 dc) in next st, hdc, sc, (3 sc) in ch-2 lp of row 1, rotate piece to work in the sc of row 1. Sc, hdc, (2 dc) in next st, ch 2, sl st in last sc. Fasten off A.

Rnd 3: Pick up B, yo and sc in the same st as first sl st of rnd 2, sc in next ch, (2 sc) in 2nd ch, 5 sc, (sc, sl st-picot, sc) in sc at tip of leaf, 5 sc, (2 sc) in next ch, sc in 2nd ch, sc in same st as last sl st of rnd 2, cut yarn and needle join to first sc of rnd.

Finishing

Weave in ends, block gently.

Flower Within a Ring

Leaf

Russian Picot Daisy

We must thank crochet writer A. Olivia Longacre Wertman for this unusual picot variation of the Russian Spoke stitch. It makes a very cute petal.

SKILL LEVEL
Intermediate

MATERIALS & TOOLS
2 or 3 colors of yarn of similar weight: center color (A), optional color for sc-row (B), sc-row and petal color (C).

Hook: Appropriate size hook to achieve a firm gauge with selected yarn, and a hook several sizes smaller.

Tapestry needle

PATTERN NOTE
Read more about the Russian Spoke stitch and its variations in the April 1900 edition of *Home Needlework Magazine*, "Relief Crochet in Silk," by A. Olivia Longacre Wertman. You can read it online for free at Google Books. The article has also been reprinted in a book called *Relief Crochet* (Lacis Publications).

FOR THESE FLOWERS WE USED

Universal Yarns Cotton Supreme (100% cotton; 3.5oz/100g = 180yd/165m): (A) color Caramel #505; (B) color Ecru #503; (C) color Hot Pink #512—medium weight yarn; ❹

GAUGE CIRCLE
(see page 11) = 1⅛"/2.8cm worked on 5.00mm (size H-8 U.S.) hook

FINISHED MEASUREMENTS
5"/12.7cm (large flower), 4¼"/10.8cm (small flower)

Blue Sky Alpacas Worsted Cotton (100% organic cotton; 3.5oz/100g = 150yd/137m): (A) color Orchid #618; (B) and (C) color Bone #80—medium weight yarn; ❹

GAUGE CIRCLE
(see page 11) = 1⅜"/3.5cm worked on 5.50mm (size I-9 U.S) hook

FINISHED MEASUREMENTS
5⅜"/13.6cm (large flower)

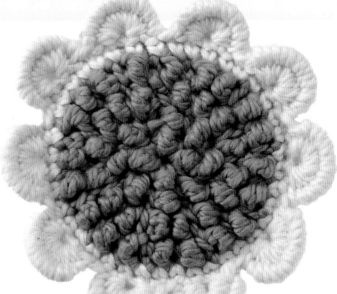

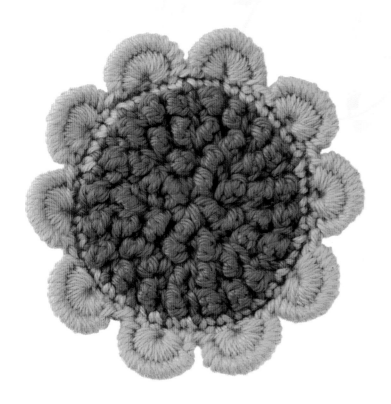

INSTRUCTIONS

Large Flower

With A, ch 5, join with sl st in first ch to form a ring.

Rnd 1: Ch 1, (sc, tr in ring) 4 times, join with sl st to first st of rnd--8 sts.

Rnd 2: Ch 1, (sc, tr) in each st around, join with sl st to first st of rnd--16 sts.

Rnd 3: Ch 1, (tr, sc) in each st around, join with sl st to first tr of rnd--32 sts.

Rnd 4: Ch 1, *(sc, tr) in next st, sc, tr, sc, (tr, sc) in next st, tr, sc, tr; rep from * 3 times, join with sl st to first st of rnd, fasten off—40 sts.

Rnd 5: Join B or C with sc in any st of rnd 4. Sc in each st around, join with sl st to first st of rnd, fasten off—40 sts.

Rnd 6: Join C in any st of rnd 5 with *sl st. Make the Russian Spoke picot as follows:

Ch 7, (hook under ch, yo, draw up a lp, yo, draw through one lp only) 14 times, sl st in next st of rnd 5 (16 lps on hook), yo and draw through all lps on hook.

With hook securely in lp, pull yarn tightly so the Russian Spoke bends over double, sl st in next 2 sts of rnd 5. Pull the last lp out a little so it won't come unraveled, then remove your hook from this lp.

One corner of the picot is still unsecured. Insert your hook in the corner st of the picot. (It is the lp that was created by the last st of the ch-7 made at the start of the picot. This lp will be tight, open it wider using a tapestry needle or a smaller crochet hook before inserting the hook into it.) Reinsert hook in the lp of the last sl st, and pull it through the picot lps. If you're pleased with how it looks, it's correct. If not, try again, or come back to it later, and see if it looks any better.

Rep from * around, cut yarn and needle join to first st of rnd--10 petals.

Small Flower

With A, work rnds 1-3 of Large Flower. Change to B or C and work rnd 5--32 sc. Change to or continue with C and work rnd 6, ending with 8 petals.

Finishing

Weave in ends, block gently.

Fleur de Lys

For the last few hundred years, the Fleur-de-Lys has been associated with France, though this stylized symbol is much older. The name "Lys" may refer to a river in northern Europe, the ancestral home of the Gauls, which was famous for its wild irises.

FOR THESE FLOWERS WE USED

Berroco Ultra® Alpaca (50% super fine alpaca, 50% Peruvian wool; 3.5oz/100g = 215yd/198m): (A) color yellow #6225; (B) color violet #6219; (C) color green #6273--light weight yarn; (3)

GAUGE CIRCLE
(see page 11) = 1"/2.5cm worked on 4.00mm (size G-6 U.S.) hook

FINISHED MEASUREMENTS
6¼"/15.9cm x 6¼"/15.9cm

Louet KidLin (49% linen, 35% kid mohair, 16% nylon; 1.75oz/50g = 250yd/228m): (A) color Mexican Orange #06; (B) color Violet #52; (C) color Grasshopper #33—fine weight yarn; (2)

GAUGE CIRCLE
(see page 11) = ¾"/1.8cm worked on 3.50mm (size E-4 U.S.) hook

FINISHED MEASUREMENTS
5"/12.7cm x 5¼"/13.4cm

SKILL LEVEL
Experienced

MATERIALS & TOOLS
3 colors of yarn of similar weight: inner petal color (A), outer petal color (B), and greenery color (C)

Hook: Appropriate size hook to achieve a firm gauge with selected yarn

Stitch markers

Tapestry needle

SPECIAL ABBREVIATIONS
Htr (half treble crochet): Yo 2 times, insert hook in st and draw up a loop (4 loops on hook), yo and draw through 2 loops (3 loops on hook), yo and draw through 3 loops (1 loop left on hook).

Hdc2tog: Half double crochet 2 stitches together

Sc-join: Holding the pieces to be joined with wrong sides together, insert hook in the front piece, then in the corresponding stitch of the other piece. Yo, pull up a loop, yo, pull through both loops on hook. This completes a sc, which holds the two pieces together.

Sl st-picot: Ch 3, sl st in base of chain.

INSTRUCTIONS

Side Petal 1

Rnd 1: With A, ch 28, hdc in 3rd ch from hook, hdc, [(2 hdc) in next st, 2 hdc] twice, (2 hdc) in next st, 11 sc, [(2 sc) in next st, sc] twice, sk 1 ch, sl st in last ch to create a ch-2 sp at this end. Fasten off A.

Rnd 2: In last ch-2 lp, join B with 3 sc, sl st-picot, sc. Working in free lps of the original ch of rnd 1, (sc2tog) twice, 3 sc, 5 sl sts, 2 sc, (hdc2tog, hdc) twice, hdc2tog, dc, (2 dc) in next st, (2 dc) in first st of turning ch.

Ch 7, sc in 3rd ch from hook, hdc2tog, 2 dc, sl st in first st of turning ch (where there are already 2 sts), ch 2, remove hook from st, going backwards for a moment,

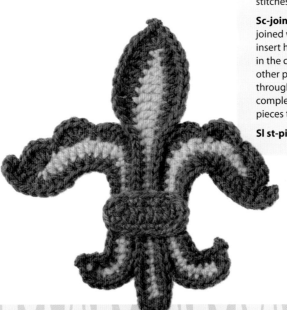

sk the dc just made and insert hook in the next to last dc, insert hook in loose ch, and pull the st through the top of the dc (curly point made).

Dc in next ch of turning ch, (5 htr) in next st, sk 1 st, sl st, sk 1 st, (6 dc) in next st, sk 1 st, sl st, sk 1 st, (4 hdc) in next st, (2 hdc) in next st, hdc, (2 hdc) in next st, 10 sc, PM in the last sc, 2 sc, [(2 sc) in next st, sc] twice, sc, cut B and needle join to first sc of rnd.

Side Petal 2

Rnd 1: With A, ch 33, hdc in 3rd ch from hook, hdc, (hdc2tog, 2 hdc) twice, hdc2tog, 11 sc, (sc2tog, sc) twice, sk 1 ch, sl st in last ch, to create a ch-2 sp at this end. Fasten off A.

Rnd 2: In last ch-2 sp, join B with sc, sl st-picot, 3 sc. Working in the free lps of the original ch of rnd 1, 2 sc, (2 sc) in next st, sc, (2 sc) in next st, 12 sc, (2 hdc) in next st, hdc, (2 hdc) in next st, PM in 2nd to last hdc, (4 hdc) in next st, sk 1 st, sl st, sk 1 st, (6 dc) in next st, sk 1 st, sl st, sk 1 st, (6 htr) in next st, dc in first st of turning ch.

Ch 4, sc in 3rd ch from hook, (2 hdc) in next st, 2 dc in side lps of last dc, (2 dc) in 2nd st of turning ch (curly point made).

(2 dc) in next st, dc, (hdc2tog, hdc) twice, hdc2tog, 2 sc, 5 sl st, 3 sc, (sc2tog) twice, cut B and needle join to first sc of rnd.

Middle Petal

Rnd 1: With A, ch 33. Sc in 3rd ch from hook, hdc, dc, htr, 4 tr, htr, dc, hdc, 18 sc, sk 1 ch, sl st in last ch to create a ch-2 sp at this end. Fasten off A.

Rnd 2: In last ch-2 sp, join B with 2 sc, sl st-picot, 2 sc. Working in free lps of the original ch of rnd 1, sc, 4 hdc.

Pick up Side Petal 1 and place its WS against the back of your work. Insert hook in next st of Middle Petal and in marked st of Side Petal 1, complete a sc-join. In each st of both pieces, work 13 more sc-joins.

Continuing on Middle Petal only, hdc, dc, htr, 6 tr, htr, (2 dc, sl st-picot, 2 dc) in ch-2 sp at top of petal, htr, 6 tr, htr, dc, hdc.

Pick up Side Petal 2 and place its WS against the back of your work. Join to Middle Petal as for Side Petal 1. Continuing on Middle Petal only, 4 hdc, sc, cut yarn and needle join to first sc of rnd.

Oval Decoration

Rnd 1: With C, ch 12, dc in 4th ch from hook, 5 dc, sk 2 ch, sl st in last ch.

Rnd 2: Continuing in same direction, ch 1, (2 sc) in same st as sl st, (2 sc) in each of rem 2 ch. Working in free lps of original ch, along bottom edge of rnd 1, 6 sc, (2 sc) in each of the next 3 ch, 6 sc. Leaving a long tail for sewing, cut yarn and needle join to first st of rnd.

Stem (optional)

With C, ch desired length of stem plus 8 sts. Hdc in 3rd ch from hook and in each rem ch. Fasten off, leaving a long tail for sewing.

Finishing

Weave in ends, except for long tail for sewing.

Block the flower with lots of steam, carefully pressing the sc-join ridges away from the center. Pin the points and edges down and let cool. Sew Oval Decoration on top of petals, using photo as a guide for placement. If necessary, block again.

Optional

Sew stem to back of middle petal of the Fleur-de-Lys.

European Rose

My family saw this rose carved into stone buildings and wrought into iron gates when we lived in Yorkshire. The symbol has been known in Europe for centuries in mythology, as the Alchemical Rose, Martin Luther's Rose, and of course, the Tudor Rose.

SKILL LEVEL
Intermediate

MATERIALS & TOOLS
4 colors of yarn of similar weight: cone color (A), two petal colors (B and C), greenery color (D)

Hook: Appropriate size hook to achieve a firm gauge with selected yarn

Stuffing

Tapestry needle

SPECIAL ABBREVIATIONS
BPsc (Back Post single crochet): Yo, insert hook from back to front between the stitch you just finished and the next stitch. Push your hook to the back between the next stitch and the stitch after that. Yo, draw up a loop which will come around the front of the stitch, yo, draw through both loops.

Hdc2tog: Half double crochet 2 stitches together.

Sl st-picot: Ch 3, sl st in base of chain.

PATTERN NOTE
The pattern is written for 4 colors, but you may choose to use only 2 or 3 colors. The tops of the petals, crocheted in rnds 5 and 8 are meant to bend over to the front.

FOR THESE FLOWERS WE USED

Lion Brand Recycled Cotton (74% recycled cotton, 24% acrylic, 2% other fiber; 3.5oz/100g = 185yd/169m): (A and B) color Seagrass #130; (C and D) color Rose Coral #205— medium weight yarn;

GAUGE CIRCLE
(see page 11) = 1¹⁄₁₆"/2.7cm worked on 4.00mm (size G-6 U.S.) hook

FINISHED MEASUREMENTS
4½"/11.4cm

Lion Brand Vanna's Glamour™ (96% acrylic, 4% metallic polyester; 1.75oz/50g = 202yd/185m): (A and B) color Platinum #150; (C) color Diamond #100; (D) color Ruby Red #113— fine weight yarn; (2)

GAUGE CIRCLE
(see page 11) = ¹³⁄₁₆"/2.1cm worked on 3.50mm (size E-4 U.S.) hook

FINISHED MEASUREMENTS
3½"/8.9cm

Dale of Norway Falk (100% superwash wool; 1¾oz/50g = 116yd/106m): (A) color Goldenrod #2427; (B) color Lime #8817; (C and D) color Off White #0017—light weight yarn; (3)

GAUGE CIRCLE
(see page 11) = 1"/2.5cm worked on 4.00mm (size G-6 U.S.) hook

FINISHED MEASUREMENTS
4¼"/10.8cm

Prism Symphony (80% merino, 10% cashmere, 10% nylon; 2oz/56g = 118yd/107m): (A and B) color Moss; (C and D) color Lipstick--medium weight yarn; (4)

GAUGE CIRCLE
(see page 11) = 1"/2.5cm worked on 4.00mm (size G-6 U.S.) hook

FINISHED MEASUREMENTS
4¼"/10.8cm

INSTRUCTIONS

Flower

With A, ch 6, join with sl st in first ch to form a ring.

Rnd 1: Ch 4 (counts as tr), 19 tr in ring, cut yarn and needle join to first st of rnd. (Or if you are not going to change colors, join with sl st to first st of rnd, ch 1)—20 tr.

Rnd 2: Join B with BPsc around the next st, BPsc around each rem st of rnd 1, including the ch-4, join with sl st to first sc of rnd.

Rnd 3: *Ch 6, sl st in 4th ch from hook, working along ch, sc and hdc, sl st in next st of rnd 2. Ch 4, sk 2 sts, sl st in next st; rep from * 4 times. Fasten off B—5 sepals and ch-4 sps and 2 skipped sts between them.

Rnd 4: Join C and *(sl st, ch 2, 5 dc, ch 2, sl st) all in next ch-4 sp, push the pointy sepal you made in rnd 3 to the front of your work and ch 1 behind it; rep from * 4 times.

Rnd 5: *Sl st in next ch-4 sp, sc in each of 2 ch going up the side of the petal, working in FL only across the top of the petal, (sc, hdc) in next st, hdc2tog, sl st-picot. The last st of the dec is in the 3rd

dc of the petal. Hdc2tog again, placing the first st of the dec in the 3rd dc of the petal. Now the 3rd dc has 2 sts in it. (Hdc, sc) in next st, sc in each of 2 ch going down the side of the petal, sl st in ch-4 sp, leaving the yarn at the back of your work, bring hook in front of the sepal to make the next st. Rep from * 4 times. Sl st in the next ch-4 sp, fasten off C.

Rnd 6: Fold petals and sepals to the front of your work as you work this rnd. Join B with *dc in the first of the 2 skipped sts under next petal (these sts are from rnd 2). Ch 8, sl st in 4th ch from hook, working down ch, sc, 3 hdc, dc in next skipped st of rnd 2, ch 7; rep from * 4 times, join with sl st to first dc of rnd. Fasten off B.

Rnd 7: Join D and *(sl st, ch 3, 9 tr, ch 3, sl st) all in next ch-7 sp, push the pointy sepal you made in rnd 6 to the front of the work and ch 1 behind it. Rep from * 4 times.

Rnd 8: *Sl st in next ch-7 sp, sc in each of 3 ch going up side of petal, working in FL only across the top of petal, sc, 2 hdc, hdc2tog, sl st-picot. The last st of the

dec is in the 5th tr of the petal. Hdc2tog again, placing the first st of the dec in the 5th tr of the petal. Now the 5th tr has 2 sts in it. 2 hdc, sc, sc in each of 3 ch going down the side of the petal, sl st in ch-7 sp, leaving the yarn in the back of the work, bring hook in front of the sepal to make the next st. Rep from * 4 times. Sl st in next ch-7 sp, then fasten off C.

Finishing

Weave in ends, wet block or gently steam block, stretching out the sepals and allowing the tops of the petals to bend over.

Cut-Out Leaf

Years ago, I sewed myself a shirt from a turquoise and white fabric with a decorative paper-cut style of tropical flowers and leaves. I tried to capture that positive-negative space feeling in these leaves.

INSTRUCTIONS

Delicate Leaf

Row 1: With A, ch 11, sl st in 5th ch from hook, (ch 2, sk 2, sl st) twice. Turn.

Row 2: Ch 4, 2 dc-CL in first ch-2 sp, ch 2, 2 tr-CL in next ch-2 sp, ch 2, (2 tr-CL, ch 5, 2 tr-CL, ch 5, 2 tr-CL) in ch-5 lp, ch 2. Working along other side of row 1, 2 tr-CL in next ch-2 sp, ch 2, 2 dc-CL in last ch-2 sp, ch 4, sl st in last st of row 1. If you're changing colors, fasten off. If not, continue with A. Do not turn.

Row 3: Join B or continue with A, and continuing around the bottom edge of the leaf, 3 sc in ch-4 sp, sc in top of first CL, (3 sc in next ch 2-sp, sc in top of next CL) twice, (4 sc, hdc) in ch-5 sp, (dc, sl st-picot, dc) in top of next CL. Working along other side of leaf, (hdc, 4 sc) in ch-5 sp, sc in top of next CL, (3 sc in next ch 2-sp, sc in top of next CL) twice, 3 sc in ch-4 sp. To make stem, ch 5, sc in 2nd ch from hook, sl st in rem ch sts, needle join to first st of rnd.

Robust Leaf

Row 1: Ch 11, sl st in 5th ch from hook, (ch 2, sk 2, sl st) twice. Turn.

Delicate Leaves

SKILL LEVEL
Intermediate

MATERIALS & TOOLS
1 or 2 colors of yarn of similar weight: main color (A), outline color (B)

Hook: Appropriate size hook to achieve a firm gauge with selected yarn

Tapestry needle

SPECIAL ABBREVIATIONS
2 dc-CL: Yo, insert hook in next stitch, yo and draw up a loop, yo, draw through 2 loops on hook; yo, insert hook in next stitch, yo and draw up a loop, yo, draw through 2 loops on hook; yo, draw through all 3 loops on hook, ch 1 to close the CL.

3 dc-CL: Yo, insert hook in next stitch, yo and draw up a loop, yo, draw through 2 loops on hook; (yo, insert hook in next stitch, yo and draw up a loop, yo, draw through 2 loops on hook) 2 times; yo, draw through all loops on hook, ch 1 to close the CL.

2 tr-CL: (Yo twice, insert hook in stitch or ring, yo and draw up a loop, yo and pull through 2 loops, yo and draw through 2 loops) twice. Yo and draw through all lps on hook.

3 tr-CL: (Yo twice, insert hook in stitch or ring, yo and draw up a loop, yo and pull through 2 loops, yo and draw through 2 loops) three times. Yo and draw through all lps on hook.

Sl st-picot: Ch 3, sl st in base of chain.

FOR THESE LEAVES WE USED

Berroco Pure® Pima (100% pima cotton, 1.75oz/50g = 115yd/106m): (A and B) color dark teal #2263, color green #2265—light weight yarn;

GAUGE CIRCLE
(see page 11) = ¹⁵⁄₁₆"/2.4cm worked on 4.00mm (size G-6 U.S.) hook

FINISHED MEASUREMENTS
2"/5.1cm x 3½"/9cm

Prism Tulle (100% nylon, 1oz/28g = 96yd/87m): (A and B) color Nevada—medium weight yarn; DO NOT BLOCK THIS YARN

GAUGE CIRCLE
(see page 11) = 1"/2.5cm worked on 5.50mm (size I-9 U.S.) hook

FINISHED MEASUREMENTS
2¼"/5.2cm x 3⅞"/9.8cm (with stem)

Yummy Yarns Jelly Yarn Fine (100% vinyl; 7oz/200g = 85yd/75m): (A and B) color Green Peppermint Glow (glows in the dark!)—medium weight yarn;

GAUGE CIRCLE
(see page 11) = 1"/2.5cm worked on 4.00mm (size G-6 U.S.) hook

FINISHED MEASUREMENTS
2⅛"/5.4cm x 3⅝"/5.2cm

Row 2: Ch 4, 3 dc-CL in first ch-2 sp, ch 2, 3 tr-CL in next ch-2 sp, ch 2, (3 tr-CL, ch 5, 3 tr-CL, ch 5, 3 tr-CL) in ch-5 lp, ch 2. Working along other side of row 1, 3 tr-CL in next ch-2 sp, ch 2, 3 dc-CL in last ch-2 sp, ch 4, sl st in last st of row 1. If you are changing colors, fasten off. Otherwise continue with A. Do not turn.

Row 3: Join B or continue with A, and continuing around bottom edge of the leaf, 3 sc in ch-4 sp, sc in top of first CL, (3 sc in next ch 2-sp, sc in top of next CL)

twice, (4 sc, hdc) in ch-5 sp, (dc, sl st-picot, dc) in top of next CL. Working along other side of leaf, (hdc, 4 sc) in ch-5 sp, sc in top of next CL, (3 sc in next ch 2-sp, sc in top of next CL) twice, 3 sc in ch-4 sp. To make stem, ch 5, sc in 2nd ch from hook, sl st in rem ch, needle join to first st of rnd.

Finishing
Weave in ends. Block.

Robust
Leaves

Maple Leaf

O Canada! Your striking flag inspired me to crochet a Maple leaf.

SKILL LEVEL
Intermediate

MATERIALS & TOOLS
1 yarn of your choice in a leafy color

Hook: Appropriate size hook to achieve a firm gauge with selected yarn

Tapestry needle

PATTERN NOTE
The Maple Leaf starts by working across one side of the chain and then its other side. In the following rows, crochet down one side of the leaf toward its base, then rotate the leaf so you can work up the other side. At the end of the row, turn and work toward the base again.

FOR THESE LEAVES WE USED

Berroco Ultra® Alpaca (50% super fine alpaca, 50% Peruvian wool; 3.5oz/100g = 215yd/198m): (A) color red #6234—light weight yarn;

GAUGE CIRCLE
(see page 11) = 1"/2.5cm worked on 4.00mm (size G-6 U.S.) hook

FINISHED MEASUREMENTS
4½"/11.4cm x 4⅝"/11.8cm (with stem)

Universal Yarns Fibra Natura Exquisite Bamboo (77% bamboo, 23% superwash merino wool; 1.76oz/50g = 109yd/100m): (A) color Sable #40-156—medium weight yarn;

GAUGE CIRCLE
(see page 11) = ⅞"/2.2cm worked on 4mm (size G-6 U.S.) hook

FINISHED MEASUREMENTS
4⅛"/10.5cm x 4⅜"/11.1cm (with stem)

Fiber Fanatic Hand Painted Yarn (100% wool, 3.5oz/100g = 245yd/223m): (A) color Sunset—medium weight yarn;

GAUGE CIRCLE
(see page 11) = 1⅜"/3.5cm worked on 5.00mm (size H-8 U.S.) hook

FINISHED MEASUREMENTS
5¼"/13.3cm x 5½"/14cm (with stem)

Brooks Farm Yarns Duet (55% kid mohair, 45% fine wool; 8oz/225g = 500yd/455m): (A) color shaded reds and gold—light weight yarn;

GAUGE CIRCLE
(see page 11) = ⅞"/2.2cm worked on 4.00mm (size G-6 U.S.) hook

FINISHED MEASUREMENTS
5"/12.7cm x 5⅛"/13cm (with stem)

INSTRUCTIONS

Leaf
Ch 12.

Row 1: Working in 1 lp of each ch, sc in 3rd ch from hook, dc, tr, 2 dc, 2 hdc, 3 sc, ch 2, rotate. Working in the unused lps along the other side of the ch, 6 sc, (sc, hdc) in next st. Ch 3, turn.

Row 2: Sk 3 ch, 8 sc, sc in ch-2 lp, ch 2, rotate. Working along the other side of the leaf, 6 sc, (sc, hdc) in next st. Ch 3, turn.

Row 3: Sk 3 ch, 8 sc, sc in ch-2 lp, ch 2, rotate. Working along the other side of the leaf, 2 sc, hdc, (hdc, dc) in next st. Ch 5, turn.

Row 4: Sc in 3rd ch from hook, sc in each of next 2 ch, 5 sc, sc in ch-2 lp, ch 2, rotate. Working along the other side of the leaf, 2 sc, hdc, (hdc, dc) in next st. Ch 5, turn.

Row 5: Sc in 3rd ch from hook, sc in each of next 2 ch, 5 sc, sc in ch-2 lp, ch 2, rotate. Working along the other side of the leaf, 8 sc. Ch 5, turn.

Row 6: Sc in 3rd ch from hook. Working in ch, dc, tr. Continuing down the edge of the leaf, tr, 3 dc, 2 hdc, 2 sc, sc in ch-2 lp, ch 2, rotate. Working along the other side of the leaf, 8 sc. Ch 5, turn.

Row 7: Sc in 3rd ch from hook. Working in ch, dc, tr. Continuing down the edge of the leaf, tr, 3 dc, 2 hdc, 2 sc, sc in ch-2 lp, ch 2, rotate. Working along the other side of the leaf, 7 sc, (sc, hdc) in next st. Ch 3, turn.

Row 8: Sk 3 ch, 9 sc, sc in ch-2 lp, ch 2, rotate. Working along the other side of the leaf, 7 sc, (sc, hdc) in next st. Ch 3, turn.

Row 9: Pay attention on this row; it's different. Sk 3 ch, 9 sc, sc in ch-2 lp, 3 sc, (hdc, dc) in next st. Ch 4, turn.

Row 10: Sl st in 3rd ch from hook, 3 sc, 3 sl sts, 3 sc, (hdc, dc) in next st, ch 4, turn.

Row 11: Sl st in 3rd ch from hook, 3 sc, 3 sl sts.

Make a stem: Ch 7, sc in 2nd ch from hook, sl st in rem ch, needle join to base of leaf.

Finishing
Weave in ends. Block.

Forget Me Not

The first live Forget-Me-Not I ever saw was in England. Who could forget such sweet flowers? Sky blue petals and yellow centers are their hallmarks, but you can crochet this flower in the colors of your choice.

FOR THESE FLOWERS WE USED

Anchor Embroidery Floss (100% cotton; 8.8yd/8m): (A and B) color white #884; (C) color shaded pinks #884—embroidery floss; **(1)**

GAUGE CIRCLE
(see page 11) = ⅝"/1.5cm worked on 3.50mm (size 00 steel U.S.) hook

FINISHED MEASUREMENTS
1¾"/4.4cm

DMC Embroidery Floss (100% cotton; 8.8yd/8m): (A) color yellow #444, (B) color blue #809 or white #5200, (C) color blue #809 or darker blue #791—embroidery floss; **(1)**

GAUGE CIRCLE
(see page 11) = ⅝"/1.5cm worked on 3.50mm (size 00 steel U.S.) hook

FINISHED MEASUREMENTS
1¾"/4.4cm

Dale of Norway Falk (100% superwash wool; 1¾oz/50g = 116yd/106m): (A) color Goldenrod #2427, (B) color Aquamarine #6604, (C) color Cerulean #6215—light weight yarn; **(3)**

GAUGE CIRCLE
(see page 11) = 1"/2.5cm worked on 4.00mm (size G-6 U.S.) hook

FINISHED MEASUREMENTS
2¾"/7cm

SKILL LEVEL
Experienced

MATERIALS & TOOLS
3 colors of yarn of similar weight: center color (A), pale petal color (B), dark petal color (C)

Hook: Appropriate size hook to achieve a firm gauge with selected yarn

Tapestry needle

SPECIAL ABBREVIATION
Htr (half treble crochet): Yo 2 times, insert hook in stitch and draw up a loop (4 loops on hook), yo and draw through 2 loops (3 loops on hook), yo and draw through 3 loops (1 loop on hook).

INSTRUCTIONS

Flower

With A, ch 4, join with sl st in first ch to form a ring.

Rnd 1: Ch 1, 10 sc in ring, cut yarn and needle join to first sc of rnd.

Rnd 2: This rnd is worked in FL only of rnd 1. Join B with dc in FL of any st of rnd 1, (ch 2, tr, ch 2, dc, ch 1) in the same st as the first dc. *Sk 1 st of previous rnd, (dc, ch 2, tr, ch 2, dc, ch 1) in the next st; rep from * 3 times. Cut yarn and needle join

over top of first st of rnd—5 groups of sts separated at the top by a ch-1 sp; at the bottom, the groups are separated by sc, which have no sts in them yet. I will refer to these as the free sc.

Rnd 3: This rnd is worked in BL only of rnd 1. Join C with sc in BL of one of the free sc of rnd 1, *(2 sc) in next st, sc in next free sc; rep from * 3 more times, (2 sc) in next st. Join with sl st in first st of rnd. The free sc now each have 1 sc in them, but are still refered to as the free sc.

Rnd 4: Ch 1, with lp still on it, bring hook to the front of the flower and insert in the free sc under the st just joined, catching both lps at top of rnd 1. Yo and pull up a lp, yo and finish the sc so that it covers the first st of rnd 3 and the ch-1 between the clusters of rnd 2. *When working the next group of sts, insert hook in next st of rnd 3, between the dc and tr of rnd 2; (hdc, dc, htr) all in the same st, catching the ch-2 sp of rnd 3 inside the sts, 2 dc in

next tr of rnd 2. In next st of rnd 3, insert hook between the tr and dc of rnd 2, (htr, dc, hdc) all in the same st, catching the ch-2 sp of rnd 2 under the sts. Sc in the next free sc of rnd 1, covering the st from rnd 3 and the ch-1 sp from rnd 2 in the st; rep from * 3 more times. Insert hook in the next st of rnd 3, between the dc and tr of rnd 2; (hdc, dc, htr) all in the same st, catching the ch-2 sp of rnd 3 inside the sts, 2 dc in the next tr of rnd 2. Insert hook between the tr and dc of rnd 2, (htr, dc, hdc) all in the next st of rnd 3, catching the ch-2 sp of rnd 2 inside the sts. Needle join over top of the first st of rnd.

Variation

If you want rnds 1 and 2 to be the same color, as in the pink and white flower shown, use this variation:

In center color, ch 4, join with sl st in first ch to form a ring.

Rnd 1: Ch 1, 10 sc in ring, Join with sl st to first st of rnd. Do not cut yarn.

Rnd 2: This rnd is worked in FL only of rnd 1. Ch 5 (counts as dc and 2 ch), (tr, ch 2, dc, ch 1) in the same st as the first dc. *Sk 1 st of previous rnd, (dc, ch 2, tr, ch 2, dc, ch 1) in the next st; rep from * 3 times. Cut

yarn and needle join over top of first st of rnd—5 groups of sts separated at the top by a ch-1 sp; at the bottom, the groups are separated by sc, which have no sts in them yet. These are the free sc.

Work rnds 3 and 4 as above in desired petal color (white is shown here).

Finishing

Weave in ends, block.

Peacock & Poppycock

The handsome peacock lends elegance to the gardens of the world with his brilliant jewel-tone or white tail feathers. His friend the poppycock, made from spare parts, is completely silly.

FOR THESE BIRDS WE USED

Cascade Luna (100% Peruvian cotton; 1.75oz/50g = 82yd/75m): (A) color green #755; (B) color blue-green #714; (C) color turquoise #754; (D) color light blue #725—medium weight yarn; (4)

GAUGE CIRCLE
(see page 11) = 1 5/16"/3.3cm worked on 6.00mm (size J-10 U.S.) hook

FINISHED MEASUREMENTS
7¾"/19.7cm x 6½"/16.5cm

Berroco Ultra® Alpaca (50% super fine alpaca, 50% Peruvian wool; 3.5oz/100g = 215yd/198m): (A and D) color teal #6285; (B) color royal blue #6260; (C) color green #6262—light weight yarn; (3)

GAUGE CIRCLE
(see page 11) = 1"/2.5cm worked on 4.00mm (size G-6 U.S.) hook

FINISHED MEASUREMENTS
5¾"/14.6cm x 5¼"/13.3cm

Caron International Naturally Caron Spa (25% rayon, 75% microdenier acrylic; 3oz/85g = 251yd/230m): (A) color Soft Sunshine #0003; Crest color Rose Bisque #0001; Tail colors Soft Sunshine #0003 and Ocean Spray #0005— light weight yarn; (3)

GAUGE CIRCLE
(see page 11) = ⅞"/2.2cm worked on 4.00mm (size G-6 U.S.) hook

FINISHED MEASUREMENTS
6"/15.3cm x 4⅜"/11.2cm (your measurements may vary depending on which pieces you choose for the crest and tail feathers)

SKILL LEVEL
Intermediate

MATERIALS & TOOLS
4 colors (or desired number) of similar weight yarn: (A) body color, (B, C, and D) tail colors

Hook: Appropriate size hook to achieve a firm gauge with selected yarn, and a hook several sizes smaller.

Tapestry needle

SPECIAL ABBREVIATION
FPdc (Front Post double crochet): Yo, insert hook from front to back between the stitch you just finished and the next stitch. Push hook to the front between the next stitch and the stitch after that. At this point, you'll see your hook across the back of the next stitch, and the top of the stitch which you would normally crochet into (but not this time), is pushed away from you. Yo, draw up a loop, which will come around the back of the stitch, (yo, draw through 2 loops) twice.

FPslst (Front Post slip stitch): Work a slip stitch (instead of a dc) in same manner as FPdc.

Hdc2tog: Half double crochet 2 stitches together.

Sl st-picot: Ch 3, sl st in base of chain.

Sc-hdc-tog: Insert hook in next stitch, yo and draw up a loop, yo and insert hook in next st, yo and draw up a loop (4 loops on hook), yo and draw through remaining loops on hook.

PATTERN NOTE
Change colors as desired.

Peacock

Peacock

INSTRUCTIONS

Right-Facing Body
With A, ch 8.

Row 1: (2 dc) in 4th ch from hook, (2 dc) in next st, sk 2 ch, sl st in last ch, turn.

Row 2: Ch 3, PM in the last ch st, dc into same st as last sl st, (2 dc) in each of the next 4 sts, (2 dc) into next ch st, turn.

Row 3 and Head: Ch 3, dc in first st, *(2 dc) in next st, dc; rep from * 4 times, (2 dc) in marked st, ch 9, (sc, hdc) in 2nd ch from hook, (2 dc) in next st, (2 hdc) in next st, 3 hdc, dc2tog, sl st in marked st, remove marker and fasten off.

OUTLINE PLUS LEGS, BEAK, AND CREST
Join A or desired yarn with sl st in the 3rd st of the ch-3 sp at the tail corner of the bird, opposite the base of the neck. Adjusting your tension as necessary to keep the work nice and flat, 9 sl sts around to leg position, continue with legs as follows:

LEGS
*Ch 10, sl st in 3rd ch from hook, sk 3 ch, sl st in rem ch, sl st in same dc as before, sl st in next st; rep from * once. 7 sl sts up chest, then working along the free lps of the ch that forms the neck, 8 sl sts, sl st in turning ch, continue with beak:

BEAK
Ch 3, sl st in 3rd ch from hook, sl st in sc and hdc of head, continue with crest:

CREST
All in next st: (sl st, ch 2, sl st-picot, hdc, sl st-picot, hdc, sl st-picot, ch 2, sl st).

Working down back of neck, 7 sl sts, sl st in same sp as last sl st of row 3.

Work 9-10 sl sts evenly spaced across the back (add or subtract 1 if it looks better on your bird). Make your sts the same size as the sts going around the bottom edge of the bird, and then sl st in the most convenient place (if you sl st in every available st, the sts will be too small). Sl st in the first sl st of rnd. Fasten off.

Left Facing Body
With A, ch 8.

Row 1: (2 dc) in 4th ch from hook, (2 dc) in next st, sk 2 ch, sl st in last ch, turn.

Row 2: Ch 3, PM in the last ch st, dc into same st as last sl st, (2 dc) in each of the next 4 sts, (2 dc) into next ch st, turn.

Head and Row 3: Ch 11, beg in 2nd ch from hook, sc-hdc-tog, dc2tog, hdc2tog, 3 hdc, (2 dc) in last ch. Working around body, *(2 dc) in next st, dc; rep from * 5 times. (2 dc) in next st, twice. Fasten off.

OUTLINE PLUS CREST, BEAK, AND LEGS
Join A or desired yarn with sl st in the first free lp of the ch at the base of the neck (this already has 2 dc in it). Working in the free lps of the ch up the back of the neck, 7 sl sts, adjusting tension as necessary to keep the work nice and flat, continue with crest as follows:

CREST
In next st work (sl st, ch 2, sl st-picot, hdc, sl st-picot, hdc, sl st-picot, ch 2, sl st), continue with beak:

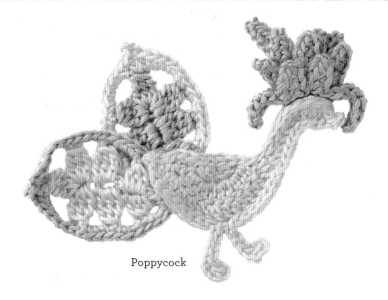

Poppycock

BEAK

Sl st in hdc and sc of the bird's head, ch 3, sl st in 3rd ch from hook, sl st in the turning ch. Working in each st down the front of the bird's neck, 2 sl sts, sk 1 st, 5 sl sts, continue with legs:

LEGS

Continuing in the same direction, 8 sl sts around the body of the bird. *Ch 7, sl st in 3rd ch from hook, ch 3, sl st in next st of original ch, and in each of rem ch, sl st in same dc as before, sl st in next st; rep from * once. 8 sl sts to point of tail end, ch 1, then 10 sl sts evenly spaced across the back. Make your sts the same size as the sts going around the bottom edge of the bird, and then sl st in the most convenient place (if you sl st in every available st, the sts will be too small). Stop 1 st short of the neck, cut yarn and needle join to first sl st of rnd.

Peacock Tail

With B, ch 4, join with sl st in first ch to form a ring.

Rnd 1: Ch 4 (counts as dc and ch 1), (dc, ch 1) in ring 5 times, join with sl st to 3rd ch of ch-4 at beg of rnd—6 dc and 6 ch.

Rnd 2: Ch 4 (counts as dc and ch 1), dc in same st as sl st join, ch 1, *(dc, ch 1, dc, ch 1) in next dc; rep from * 4 times, join with sl st to 3rd ch of ch-4 at beg of rnd—12 dc and 12 ch.

Rnd 3: Ch 1, FPslst around the ch-3 at beg of last rnd, ch 5 (counts as dc and ch 2), *FPdc around next dc, ch 2; rep from * 10 times, join with sl st to 3rd ch of ch-4 at beg of rnd. Fasten off.

Rnd 4: Join C with (sc, hdc, dc, hdc, sc) in same st as sl st join (shell made), sl st in ch-2 sp, *(sc, hdc, dc, hdc, sc) in next dc, sl st in ch-2 sp; rep from * 10 times, sl st in first st of rnd—12 shells.

Rnd 5: Sk 2 shells and join D with *(hdc, sl st-picot, dc, sl st-picot, dc, sl st-picot, hdc) in dc (middle st of next shell), ch 2; rep from * 6 times, then (hdc, sl st-picot, dc, sl st-picot, dc, sl st-picot, hdc) in dc (middle st of next shell – picot shell made). Fasten off—8 picot shells.

Finishing

Weave in ends. Arrange bird body on top of tail, with the point of the bird's back end at the center of the tail piece. Adjust so that one plain shell of the tail shows on either side of the bird's body, and the picot shells fan out behind. See photo for guidance. Sew the body on top of the tail.

Poppycock

Crochet the Peacock body, except do not make the crest: simply sl st in the st that would normally have the crest in it. Crochet a flower or leaf of your choice for the crest and for the tail feathers, leaving off any extra flower centers or leaf stems. Sew a motif under the bird's head for a crest, and at its tail end for tail feathers. For the crest, try folding a flower in half before sewing it to the head.

This poppycock has an Edelweiss (page 98) (minus the center clumps and folded in half) for a crest and two Robust Cut-Out Leaves (page 82) (minus stems) for the tail feathers. The Edelweiss makes great tail feathers, too.

Poinsettia

A native of Mexico, the poinsettia is a favorite Christmas holiday decoration in the United States. Its tiny yellow flowers are over-whelmed by a profusion of brilliant red leaves, made even brighter by the contrasting green leaves underneath.

FOR THESE FLOWERS WE USED

Lion Brand Vanna's Glamour™ (96% acrylic, 4% metallic polyester; 1.75oz/50g = 202yd/185m): (A) color Ruby Red #113; (B) color Platinum #150—fine weight yarn; **(2)**

GAUGE CIRCLE
(see page 11) = 13⁄16"/2.1cm worked on 3.50mm (size E-4 U.S.) hook

FINISHED MEASUREMENTS
4⅞"/12.3cm

Dale of Norway Falk (100% superwash wool; 1 3/4oz/50g = 116yd/106m): (A) color Red #4018; (B) color Fern #9155—sport weight yarn; **(3)**

GAUGE CIRCLE
(see page 11) = 1"/2.5cm worked on 4.00mm (size G-6 U.S.) hook

FINISHED MEASUREMENTS
5¾"/14.6cm

SKILL LEVEL
Experienced

MATERIALS & TOOLS
2 colors of yarn of similar weight: red for petals (A), green for leaf (B)

Hook: Appropriate size hook to achieve a firm gauge with selected yarn

Gold or yellow embellishment for flower center, such as beads, sequins, small buttons, or embroidery floss

Tapestry needle

SPECIAL ABBREVIATIONS
Htr (half treble crochet): Yo 2 times, insert hook in stitch and draw up a loop (4 loops on hook), yo and draw through 2 loops (3 loops on hook), yo and draw through 3 loops (1 loop left on hook).

Sl st-picot: Ch 3, sl st in base of chain.

Small petal: Ch 7, sl st in 3rd ch from hook; working down ch, sc, dc, (dc, sl st) in next st, sl st in last ch.

PATTERN NOTES
The Poinsettia is asymmetrical, so please read the instructions carefully.

INSTRUCTIONS
Flower
With B, ch 4, join with sl st in first ch to form a ring.

Rnd 1: Ch 2 (counts as hdc), ch 2, *hdc in ring, ch 2; rep from * 5 times, join with sl st to 2nd ch of rnd. Fasten off B—7 hdc and ch-2 sp.

Rnd 2: In any hdc of rnd 1, join A with sl st, make a Small Petal, sl st in same hdc.

In first ch-sp (Medium Petal): *Sl st in ch-sp, ch 9, sc in 4th ch from hook; working down the ch, 2 hdc, sc, ch 2, sl st in same ch-sp.* Ch 1.

In 2nd ch-sp (Large Petal): **Sl st in ch-sp, ch 10, sc in 4th ch from hook; working down the ch, hdc, dc, hdc, sc, ch 2, sl st in same ch-sp.** Ch 1.

In 3rd ch-sp (Medium Petal): Rep bet * above, sl st in next hdc, make a Small Petal, sl st in same hdc.

In 4th ch-sp (Medium Petal): Rep bet * above, sl st in next hdc, make a Small Petal, sl st in same hdc.

In 5th ch-sp (Large Petal): Rep bet ** above, ch 1.

In 6th ch-sp (Medium Petal): Rep bet * above, ch 1.

In 7th ch-sp (Large Petal): Rep bet ** above.

The Medium and Large Petals look like sticks. The next rnd finishes the Medium and Large Petals.

Rnd 3: Fold the Small Petal to the front, out of the way, ch 2 behind it.

First petal (Medium): *working up the side of the petal, 2 sc in ch-2 sp, hdc, dc, 2 htr, (htr, 2 dc, sl st-picot, 2 dc, htr) all in ch-3 lp at end of petal. Working down the other side of the petal, 2 htr, dc, hdc, 2 sc in ch-2 sp. Ch 1.*

2nd petal (Large): **working up the side of the petal, 2 sc in ch-2 sp, hdc, dc, 3 tr, (tr, 2 dc, sl st-picot, 2 dc, tr) all in ch-3 lp at end of petal. Working down the other side of the petal, 3 tr, dc, hdc, 2 sc in ch-2 sp.** Ch 1.

3rd petal (Medium): Rep bet * once. Fold Small Petal to the front, out of the way, ch 1.

4th petal (Medium): Rep bet * once. Fold Small Petal to the front, out of the way, ch 1.

5th petal (Large): Rep bet ** once, ch 1.

6th petal (Medium): Rep bet * once, ch 1.

7th petal (Large): Rep bet ** once.

Rnd 4: Fold previous petals to the front, and work this rnd behind them.

Behind the Small Petal of rnd 1, sl st in ch-2 sp, ch 10, sc in 4th ch from hook; working down the ch, hdc, dc, hdc, sc, ch 2, sl st in same ch-2 sp.

*Ch 3, sl st in next ch-1 sp between petals.

(Ch 3, sl st in ch1-sp between petals, ch 10, sc in 4th ch from hook; working down the ch, hdc, dc, hdc, sc, ch 2, sl st in same ch 1-sp) twice; rep from * once—beg of 5 unevenly-spaced Large petals.

Rnd 5: Ch 3, **working up the side of the petal, 2 sc in ch-2 sp, hdc, dc, 3 tr, (tr, 2 dc, sl st-picot, 2 dc, tr) all in ch-3 lp at end of

petal. Working down the other side of the petal, 3 tr, dc, hdc, 2 sc in ch-2 sp. **

‡ (Ch 2, sl st in next ch-3 sp) twice.

Ch 2, rep between ** and ** once.

Ch 3, rep between ** and ** once.

Rep from ‡ once.

Sl st in next ch-sp. Fasten off, leaving a long tail for sewing.

Green Leaf
With B, ch 10.

Rnd 1: Sc in 4th ch from hook, hdc, 3 dc, hdc, sc, ch 2, rotate so you are looking at the free lps of the original ch.

Rnd 2: Working in the free lps of the ch, 2 sc, hdc, dc, 2 tr; (tr, 2 dc, sl st-picot, 2 dc, tr) in ch-sp at tip of leaf; working down other side of leaf, 2 tr, dc, hdc, 2 sc, sl st in ch-2 sp at base of leaf. Fasten off, leaving a long tail for sewing.

Finishing

Pin down the tips of the petals to an ironing surface to keep them straight, and then block.

Weave in ends, except for the long tails for sewing.

Tack petals together from the back, about halfway up the petals, taking one or two stitches in each petal edge and skimming the backs of the crochet stitches only.

Sew green leaf to the underside of the flower.

Sew 3-5 beads, buttons, sequins, or French knots to the center of the flower.

Flamenco Flower

The swirling ruffles on a Spanish dancer's dress suggested this flower to me. I can imagine it as a tassel on the end of a curtain tie-back or, as you'll see, a key fob. My daughter took one look and said, "That would make a pretty Christmas tree ornament!"

FOR THESE FLOWERS WE USED

Coats & Clark Aunt Lydia's Classic Crochet Thread, No. 10, Art. 154, (100% mercerized cotton, 350yd/320m): (A) color Hot Pink #332; (B) color Black #0012; (C) color Orchid Pink #0401; (D) color Wasabi #0397—10-count crochet thread; 🔟

GAUGE CIRCLE
(see page 11) = ⅜"/0.9cm worked on 2.00mm (size 4 steel U.S.) hook

FINISHED MEASUREMENTS
1⅞"/4.8cm x 2 3/8"/6cm

Berroco Seduce® (47% rayon, 25% linen, 17% silk, 11% nylon; 1.41oz/40g = 100yd/92m): (A) color red #4445; (B and C) color purple #4474; (D) color green #4453— fine weight yarn; 🄶

GAUGE CIRCLE
(see page 11) = ¾"/1.9cm worked on 3.50mm (size E-4 U.S.) hook

FINISHED MEASUREMENTS
3"/7.5cm x 4½"/11.5cm (double flower)

SKILL LEVEL
Intermediate

MATERIALS & TOOLS
4 colors of yarn of similar weight: flower color (A), picot trim color (B), stamen color (C), and greenery color (D)

Hook: Appropriate size hook to achieve a firm gauge with selected yarn

Stuffing

Tapestry needle

SPECIAL ABBREVIATION
Sl st-picot: Ch 3, sl st in base of chain.

INSTRUCTIONS

Flower

With A, ch 4, join with sl st in first ch to form a ring.

Rnd 1: Ch 2 (counts as hdc), 11 hdc in ring, join with sl st to 2nd ch of rnd—12 hdc.

Rnd 2: Ch 2, 2 hdc, (2 hdc) in next st, *3 hdc, (2 hdc) in next st; rep from * once, join with sl st to first st of rnd—15 hdc.

Rnds 3 – 8: Ch 2, hdc in each rem st around, join with sl st to first st of rnd.

Rnd 9: Ch 2, working in BL only, hdc in each rem st around, join with sl st to first st of rnd.

Rnd 10: Ch 2, hdc, (2 hdc) in next st, *2 hdc, (2 hdc) in next st; rep from * 3 times, join with sl st to first st of rnd—20 hdc.

Ruffle Rnd 11: Ch 1, (2 sc) in each st around, join with sl st to first st of rnd—40 sc.

Ruffle Rnd 12: Ch 4 (counts as dc and ch 1), *dc in next st, ch 1, (dc, ch 1, dc, ch 1) in next st; rep from * around, ending with dc, ch 1 in last st, join with sl st to 3rd ch of ch-4 at beg of rnd. Fasten off A—60 dc and 60 ch sts.

Ruffle Rnd 13: Join B with sl st in any ch-1 sp of ruffle rnd 12. *Sl st-picot, sl st in next ch-1 sp; rep from * around, sl st-picot, cut B and needle join to first sl st of rnd—60 picots.

Ruffle Round 14: Join A in any FL of rnd 8 with (2 sc) in same st, (2 sc) in each st around, join with sl st to first st of rnd—30 sc.

Ruffle Rnd 15: Same as ruffle rnd 12, except ending with 45 dc and 45 ch.

Ruffle Rnd 16: Same as ruffle rnd 13, except ending with 45 picots.

Shape Holder

With A, ch 4, join with sl st in first ch to form a ring.

Rnd 1: Ch 2 (counts as hdc), 9 hdc in ring, join with sl st to 2nd ch of ch-2 at beg of rnd—10 hdc.

Rnds 2-7: Ch 2, hdc in each st around, join with sl st to first st of rnd.

Fasten off A after rnd 7. Lightly stuff this piece.

Stamens

With C, ch 4, join with sl st in first ch to form a ring.

Rnd 1: Ch 2 (counts as hdc), 9 hdc in ring, join with sl st to 2nd ch of ch-2 at beg of rnd—10 hdc.

Rnd 2: *Sl st in BL of next st, ch 11, working back along ch, sl st in 2nd ch from hook, (2 sc) in next st twice, 7 sl sts, sl st in BL of next st of rnd 1; rep from * 4 times, sl st in first st of rnd. Fasten off C, leaving a long tail for sewing.

Sepals and Stem

With D, ch 4, join with sl st in first ch to form a ring.

Rnd 1: *Ch 8, sc in 3rd ch from hook, hdc, 2 dc, hdc, sc, sl st in ring; rep from * 3 times. Ch 11 or desired length of stem, sc in 3rd ch from hook and in each rem ch. To secure the stem, sl st in ring between the 2nd and 3rd sepal petals. Fasten off D, leaving a long tail for sewing.

Finishing

Weave in ends except long tails for sewing.

Place the right side of the stamens on top of the shape holder's opening, like a lid. Sew the last round of the shape holder to the front loops of the stamen. Push the shape holder into the bell of the flower to help it hold its shape.

Center the sepals on the top of the flower. Catching loops from the shape holder as you go, sew the sepals and stem in place at the top and about 3 sts down from the top (a dc) of each sepal. This allows the tips of the sepals to curl up.

Wrap the flower in a very moist press cloth. Roll the wrapped flower gently on the ironing surface with a steam iron, so the flower gets very steamy but not squashed. Remove the press cloth, stretch and pull the ruffles. Pull the picots outward (mine had a tendency to curl upward). Let cool.

Any Color Pinks

The idea for this flower comes from the Turkish oya, a crocheted, needle-lace, or tatted trim. Oyas are applied to garments and home accessories with a lovely sense of balance in color and pattern. These flowers are "pinks" because of their zig-zag edges.

Flower with
Simple Stem
and Calyx

SKILL LEVEL
Intermediate

MATERIALS & TOOLS
2 colors of yarn of similar weight: flower or bud color (A), stem and leaf color (B)

Hook: Appropriate size hook to achieve a firm gauge with selected yarn

Tapestry needle

SPECIAL ABBREVIATION
Sl st-picot: Ch 3, sl st in base of chain.

PATTERN NOTE
When you crochet in the back loop of previous rows as directed in the instructions, each row forms a ridge, which gives these small flowers a pleasing texture.

FOR THESE FLOWERS WE USED

Lion Brand LB Collection Cotton Bamboo (52% cotton, 48% rayon from bamboo; 3.5oz/100g = 245yd/224m): (A) color Gardenia #170; (B) color Snapdragon #174—light weight yarn; (3)

GAUGE CIRCLE
(see page 11) = 1"/2.5cm worked on 4.00mm (size G-6 U.S.) hook

FINISHED MEASUREMENTS
4"/10.2cm x 4⅛"/10.5cm (flower with simple stem); 1"/2.5cm x 3½"/8.9cm (bud with simple stem)

Universal Yarns Fibra Natura Flax (100% linen, 1.76oz/50g = 137yd/125m): (A) color Poppy #102; (B) color Tarragon #12—light weight yarn; (3)

GAUGE CIRCLE
(see page 11) = 1³⁄₁₆"/2.1cm worked on 3.50mm (size E-4 U.S.) hook

FINISHED MEASUREMENTS
3½"/8.9cm x 4⅞"/9.8cm (flower with fancy stem); 1 1/8"/2.9cm x 3⅛"/7.9cm (bud with fancy stem)

INSTRUCTIONS

Flower

Row 1: With A, ch 12, sc in 4th ch from hook and in next 3 ch sts. Ch 1, turn--5 ch sts rem unworked.

Row 2: Sc in BL of each of the next 3 sc. Ch 4, turn.

Row 3: Sc in 4th ch from hook, sc in BL of each of the next 3 sc. Ch 1, turn.

Row 4: Sc in BL of each of the next 3 sc. Ch 4, turn.

Row 5: Sc in 4th ch from hook, sc in BL of each of the next 3 sc.

Rotate the piece one-quarter turn, so you are looking at the edge without the picots. Draw up a lp in the st that has the last sc in it. Draw up a lp in the edge of row 3 (next to the middle ridge) and in the edge of row 1 (next to the five unworked ch)--4 lps on hook. Yo and draw through all 4 lps. Tighten lp to pull rows tog.

Sc in each of rem 5 ch sts; rep rows 1-5 two more times. Fasten off and weave in ends before attaching stems.

Bud

Petal 1: With A, ch 9, sc in 3rd ch from hook (this forms a turning ch at the tip of the petal), 2 sc, sc2tog, 2 sc.

Petal 2: Ch 8, sc in 3rd ch from hook (this forms a turning ch at the tip of the petal), 5 sc.

Petal 3: Ch 5, insert hook in the turning ch of Petal 2, then insert hook in the turning ch of Petal 1. Yo, draw through all lps on hook, ch 1, sk 1 ch, sk sl st, 2 sc, (2 sc) in next st, 2 sc. Fasten off yarn and weave in ends before attaching stems.

Bud with
Simple Stem
and Calyx

Simple Stem and Calyx

With B, ch 10. Pick up the flower or bud, with RS facing and its base up so you can work into it (petals are dangling below). Work a 5 dc-CL, placing the sts as follows, being careful to work only first part of st in each (yo, insert hook in st and draw up a lp, yo and draw through 2 lps on hook), then rep for rem sts:

First st in top of last sc of the flower or bud;

2nd st in side of same sc;

3rd st in side of sc at the base of the middle petal;

4th st in side of sc at the base of the last petal;

5th st in very first ch of the flower or bud.

Let's review where you are now: you have 5 dc half-done, spread across the base of the flower or bud, with one in each edge, and one in the side of the sc at the base of each petal—6 lps on hook. Now finish the CL by yo and pull through all lps on hook, ch 1 to secure CL.

FINISH STEM

10 sl sts along original stem ch, ch 3, turn.

Make a leaf at the base of the stem: sk 3 ch, (2 dc, sl st-picot, ch 3, sl st) all in next st. Fasten off.

Fancy Stem and Calyx

Row 1: With B, ch 12, sl st-picot. Pick up the flower, RS facing and the petals up. You will be working in the base of the flower from this direction.

Insert hook, from front, in very first ch of flower. With yarn behind, yo and complete a sl st. Turn to work back along stem ch.

Row 2: 3 sc, ch 1, turn.

Row 3: Working in BL, 3 sc, sl st-picot. Insert hook in the front of the flower, between the first and 2nd sc of the middle petal. With yarn behind the flower, yo and complete a sl st. Turn to work back along the sc of the stem.

Row 4: Working in BL, 3 sc, PM in st at the base of the sc just completed, ch 1, turn.

Flower with
Fancy Stem
and Calyx

Row 5: Working in BL, 3 sc, sl st picot. Insert hook in the front of the flower, in the top of the very last sc of the last petal. With yarn behind the flower, yo and complete a sl st. Turn to work back along the sc of the stem.

Row 6: Working in BL, 3 sc. Rotate work so you are looking at the base of the calyx. Insert hook in marked st, remove marker, yo, pull up a lp. Sk 1 ch of stem, insert hook in next st, yo and draw up a lp (3 lps on hook). Yo and draw through all lps on hook.

FINISH STEM

7 sc in original stem ch. If desired, add a leaf as for the Simple Calyx and Stem. Fasten off.

Finishing

Weave in ends and block.

Edelweiss

With its wooly bracts, the edelweiss seems perfectly dressed for its chilly alpine home. This irregular little plant is celebrated in the songs, stories, and folk crafts of Europe.

FOR THESE FLOWERS WE USED

Earth Arts Naturally Dyed Navajo-Churro Yarn (100% wool, 4oz/113g = approximately 175yd/159m): (A) color dark cream, (B) color antique gold, (C) color spruce—bulky weight yarn; **5**

GAUGE CIRCLE
(see page 11) = 1¼"/3.1cm worked on 5.00mm (size H-8 U.S.) hook

FINISHED MEASUREMENTS
4⅛"/10.5cm (flower only, longest measurement, before felting); 4"/10cm (after felting)

Cascade 220 Wool (100% Peruvian Highland wool; 3.5oz/100g = 220yd/200m): (A) color cream #8010, (B) color yellow #9496, (C) color green #7814—medium weight yarn; **4**

GAUGE CIRCLE
(see page 11) = 1"/2.5cm worked on 4.00mm (size G-6 U.S.) hook

FINISHED MEASUREMENTS
3¼"/8.3cm (flower only, longest measurement, before felting); 3"/7.6cm (after felting)

Lion Brand Lion® Cotton (100% cotton; 5oz/142g = 236yd/215m): (A) color white #100—medium weight yarn; **4**

GAUGE CIRCLE
(see page 11) = 1⁵⁄₁₆"/3.3cm worked on 5.00mm (size H-8 U.S.) hook

Sewing thread and Mill Hill Beads

FINISHED MEASUREMENTS
4⅜"/11.1cm (flower only)

SKILL LEVEL
Easy

MATERIALS & TOOLS
2 to 3 colors of yarn of similar weight: white or cream for flower (A), yellow for center (B), optional pale green (C)

Hook: Appropriate size hook to achieve a firm gauge with selected yarn

Tapestry needle

6 or 7 beads for center

Sewing thread or a single strand of embroidery flossof previous rows as directed in the instructions, each row forms a ridge, which gives these small flowers a pleasing texture.

INSTRUCTIONS

Flower

With A, ch 4, join with sl st in first ch to form a ring.

Rnd 1: Ch 3 (counts as dc), 9 dc in ring, join with sl st in top of first ch-3 to form a ring—10 dc.

Rnd 2: Ch 8, sc in 3rd ch from hook, hdc, 4 dc, sk 1 st of rnd 1, sl st in FL of next st. (Ch 5, sc in 3rd ch from hook, 2 hdc, sl st in next st of rnd 1) twice. Ch 7, sc in 3rd ch from hook, 4 hdc, sk 1 st of rnd 1, sl st in FL of next st. Ch 10, sc in 3rd ch from hook, 7 hdc, sk 1 st of rnd 1, sl st in FL of next st. Ch 7, sc in 3rd ch from hook, 4 hdc, sk 1 st of rnd 1, sl st in first st of rnd— 6 irregular petals.

Rnd 3: Fold petals of rnd 2 to the front, out of the way. Sl st in BL of next st, *ch 6, sc in 3rd ch from hook, 3 hdc, sk 1 st of rnd 1, sl st in BL of next st. Ch 7, sc in 3rd ch from hook, 4 hdc, sk 1 st of rnd 1, sl st in BL of next st; rep from * once. Ch 6, sc in 3rd ch from hook, 3 hdc, sk 1 st of rnd 1, sl st in first st of rnd. Fasten off—5 irregular petals.

Leaf (optional)
With C, ch 9, sc in 3rd ch from hook, 6 hdc, fasten off. Arrange leaf as you like at the back of the flower and sew in place.

Center
The flowering part of the edelweiss comprises 6 or 7 clumps in the center. One clump is central, and the other 5 or 6 are gathered around it, evenly or unevenly spaced.

Embroidered clumps
Using B, make 6 or 7 French knots spaced as described above. Or make small Xs of satin stitch on the dc center of the flower. You can enhance your embroidery with bits of commercial wool felt or craft felt.

Bead clumps
Use sewing thread or embroidery floss to sew 6 to 7 beads or bead clusters onto flower. Separate floss if necessary to get the correct thickness.

Needle-felted clumps
After felting the flower (if desired), needle-felt clumps of yellow wool roving into the center of the flower. Build up the clumps as desired. Embroider small accents if desired.

Finishing
Weave in ends. Block, even if you plan to felt the flower.

If you're using feltable wool for the flower and center and leaf, make the entire flower first. Then felt in the washing machine or using your favorite felting method.

Always felt before adding beads or non-wool embroidery or crochet.

Russian Spoke Flower

A. Olivia Longacre Wertman developed the Russian Spoke Stitch as a crochet version of Russian Darning. It remained for me to figure out how to use it in a flower. This is a trans-generational joint effort.

SKILL LEVEL
Intermediate

MATERIALS & TOOLS
1 color of yarn (A)

Hook: Appropriate size hook to achieve a firm gauge with selected yarn

Stitch marker

Tapestry needle

SPECIAL ABBREVIATION
Htr (half treble crochet): Yo 2 times, insert hook into stitch and draw up a loop (4 loops on hook), yo and draw through 2 loops (3 loops on hook), yo and draw through 3 loops (1 loop left on hook).

PATTERN NOTE
When you make the Russian Spoke Stitch, before drawing the last loop through all the loops on the hook, let the yarn drop out of your hand so there is no tension on it.

FOR THESE FLOWERS WE USED
Universal Yarns Fibra Natura Exquisite Bamboo (77% bamboo, 23% superwash merino wool; 1.76oz/50g = 109yd/100m): (A) color Purple #40-667—medium weight yarn; (**4**)

GAUGE CIRCLE
(see page 11) = ⅞"/2.2cm worked on 4.00mm (size G-6 U.S.) hook

FINISHED MEASUREMENTS
4⅜"/11.1cm

Prism Kid Slique (66% rayon, 26% kid mohair, 8% nylon; 2oz/56g = 88yd/80m): (A) color Tea Rose or Ginger—bulky weight yarn; (**5**)

GAUGE CIRCLE
(see page 11) = 1¼"/3cm worked on 5.00mm (size H-8 U.S.) hook

FINISHED MEASUREMENTS
5¼"/13.3cm

DMC Cebelia, No. 10 (100% mercerized cotton; (1.75oz/50g): (A) color Peach #754—10-count crochet thread; (**0**)

GAUGE CIRCLE
(see page 11) = ½"/1.3cm worked on 2.00mm (size 4 steel U.S.) hook

FINISHED MEASUREMENTS
2⁵⁄₁₆"/5.9cm

The Back of the
Russian Spoke
Flower

INSTRUCTIONS

Flower

Ch 5, sl st in first ch to form a ring.

Rnd 1: Ch 12, PM in the first ch from hook, sc in 2nd ch from hook. From now on, work in the ch-sp (not in individual sts). *Working in the ch-sp: hdc, dc, htr, 3 tr, htr, dc, hdc, sc, sl st. Push these sts carefully back along the ch, so that about 5 ch are showing.

To make the Russian Spoke: (hook under the ch, yo, pull up a lp, yo, pull through 1 lp only) 10 times, insert hook in ring, yo and pull up a lp—12 lps on hook. Yo and draw through all lps on hook. Pull yarn out far enough that the spoke stands straight. **

The lp on hook now will remain idle for a while; keep it on hook for now. The yarn emerges from the lower end of the long spoke.

Insert hook in ring, yo and draw up a lp. Ch 11, draw last ch through the idle lp, ch **1.** Skipping the idle lp, sc around ch; rep from * 5 times.

Rep between * and **. After **, cut yarn, leaving a yarn end of about 6"/15cm. Draw the lp all the way out of the spoke. Thread yarn on tapestry needle, straighten the very first petal, and sew around the st that has the marker in it, thereby

attaching it to the last spoke. Bring needle back down through the spoke, through the same line of lps you pulled the thread out of, to the center of the flower. Adjust spoke height. Remove marker.

Finishing
Weave in ends, block.

Picot Mexico

At a Mexican market in San Antonio, Texas, we saw lively and colorful handcrafts painted with lots of dots. Using picot stitches as a substitute for dots, I hoped to capture that joyful vitality in this flower.

FOR THESE FLOWERS WE USED

Blue Sky Alpacas Skinny Dyed (100% organically grown cotton; 2.3oz/65g = 150yd/137m): (A through E) color light blue #301—light weight yarn; (3)

GAUGE CIRCLE
(see page 11) = ¹⁵⁄₁₆"/2.4cm worked on 4.00mm (size G-6 U.S.) hook

FINISHED MEASUREMENTS
5¼"/13.3cm (large flower)

Dale of Norway Baby Ull (100% superwash merino wool; 1.75oz/50g = 180yd/165m): (A) color white #0100 or yellow #2106; (B) color white #0100 or light blue #5914; (C) color light blue #5914 or medium blue #5726; (D) color medium blue #5726 or navy #5755; (E) color navy #5755 or red 4018—superfine weight yarn; (1)

GAUGE CIRCLE
(see page 11) = ¾"/1.9cm worked on 3.50mm (size E-4 U.S.) hook

FINISHED MEASUREMENTS
3¼"/8.3cm (small flower), 3⅞"/9.8cm (large flower)

Small Flower

SKILL LEVEL
Intermediate

MATERIALS & TOOLS
Up to 5 colors of yarn of similar weight: center color (A), 3 picot colors (B, C, and D), petal color (E)

Hook: Appropriate size hook to achieve a firm gauge with selected yarn

Stuffing

Tapestry needle

SPECIAL ABBREVIATIONS
BPdc (Back Post double crochet):
Yo, insert hook from back to front between the stitch you just finished and the next stitch. Push hook to the back between the next stitch and the stitch after that. At this point, you'll see your hook across the front of the next stitch, and the top of the stitch that you would normally crochet in (but not this time), is pushed toward you. Yo, draw up a loop, which will come around the front of the stitch, (yo, draw through 2 loops) twice.

BPsc (Back Post single crochet):
Work sc (instead of a dc) in same manner as BPdc.

Dtr (double treble crochet): Yo 3 times, insert hook in stitch and draw up a loop (5 loops on hook), (yo and draw through 2 loops) 4 times.

Sl st-picot: Ch 3, sl st in base of chain.

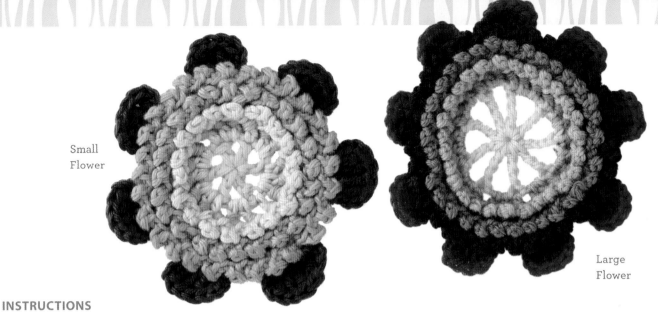

Small
Flower

Large
Flower

INSTRUCTIONS

Large Flower

With A, ch 5, join with sl st in first ch to form a ring.

Rnd 1: Ch 8 (counts as dtr and 3 ch), (dtr in ring, ch 3) 8 times, join with sl st in 5th ch of original ch-8, fasten off—9 dtr separated by ch-3 sp.

Rnd 2: Join B with dc in any dtr of previous rnd, sl st-picot, (dc, sl st-picot) twice in ch-3 sp. *Dc in next dtr, sl st-picot, (dc, sl st-picot) twice in ch-3 sp; rep from * around, join with sl st to first dc of rnd. Fasten off—27 dc and picot pairs.

Rnd 3: Join C with *(BPdc around next dc, sl st-picot) 3 times, (BPdc, sl st-picot) around the same st twice, (BPdc around next dc, sl st-picot) 4 times, (BPdc, sl st-picot) around the same st twice; rep from * around, join with sl st to first dc of rnd. Fasten off—33 dc and picot pairs.

Rnd 4: Join D with *(BPdc around next dc, sl st-picot) 10 times, (BPdc, sl st-picot) around the same st twice; rep from * around, join with sl st to first dc of rnd—36 dc and picot pairs.

Rnd 5: Continuing with D, ch 1, *BPsc around next dc, ch 1; rep from * around, join with sl st to first sc of rnd. Fasten off—72 sts.

Rnd 6: Join E in any sc of rnd 5 with *(sl st, ch 3, tr) all in same st, (2 tr) in ch-sp, (tr, ch 3, sl st) all in next sc (petal made), (sl st in next ch-sp, sl st in next sc) twice, sl st in next ch-sp; rep from * 8 times, join with sl st or needle join to first st of rnd. Fasten off—9 petals.

Small Flower

Using A, ch 5, join with sl st in first ch to form a ring.

Rnd 1: Ch 5 (counts as dc and 2 ch), (dc in ring, ch 2) 5 times, join with sl st in 3rd ch of original ch-5. Fasten off—6 dc separated by ch-3 sp.

Rnd 2: Join B with dc in any dc of previous rnd, sl st-picot, (dc, sl st-picot) twice in ch-3 sp. *Dc in next dc, sl st-picot, (dc, sl st-picot) twice in ch-3 sp; rep from * around, join with sl st to first dc of rnd. Fasten off—18 dc and picot pairs.

Rnd 3: Join C with *(BPdc around next dc, sl st-picot) 2 times, (BPdc, sl st-picot) around the same stitch twice; rep from * around, join with sl st to first dc of rnd. Fasten off—24 dc and picot pairs.

Rnd 4: Join D with *(BPdc around next dc, sl st picot) 5 times, (BPdc, sl st-picot) around the same st twice; rep from * around, join with sl st to first dc of rnd—28 dc and picot pairs.

Rnd 5: Continuing with D, ch 1, *BPsc around next dc, ch 1; rep from * around, join with sl st to first sc of rnd. Fasten off—56 sts.

Rnd 6: Join E in any sc of rnd 5 with *(sl st, ch 3, tr) in same st, (2 tr) in ch-sp, (tr, ch 3, sl st) in next sc (petal made), (sl st in next ch-sp, sl st in next sc) twice, sl st in next ch-sp; rep from * 6 times, join with sl st or needle join to first st of rnd. Fasten off—7 petals.

Finishing

Weave in ends. Block gently, stretch, pull, and if necessary, pin the petals to help them lie flat.

Anatolian King Flower

Tucked among tulips and sprays of plum blossoms on a Turkish tile panel, this curly-petal flower was called "king flower." It's probably a stylized carnation or lily, and it does have an imperial look.

FOR THESE FLOWERS WE USED

Berroco Suede® (100% nylon; 1.75oz/50g = 120yd/111m): (A) color Campfire #3739, (B) color Aloe Vera #3786—medium weight yarn; (**4**)

GAUGE CIRCLE
(see page 11) = 1"/2.5cm worked on 4.00mm (size G-6 U.S.) hook

FINISHED MEASUREMENTS
4⅞"/12.3cm x 5"/12.7cm (with calyx only), stem adds 7⅜"/18.7cm

Brooks Farm Yarns Duet (55% kid mohair, 45% fine wool; 8oz/225g = 500yd/455m): (A) color shaded reds and gold, (B) color shaded green/brown/gold—light weight yarn; (**3**)

GAUGE CIRCLE
(see page 11) = ⅞"/2.2cm worked on 4.00mm (size G-6 U.S.) hook

FINISHED MEASUREMENTS
3¾"/9.5cm x 4 3/8"/11.1cm (with calyx only), stem adds 6¾"/17.1cm

SKILL LEVEL
Intermediate

MATERIALS & TOOLS
2 colors of yarn of similar weight: flower color (A), greenery color (B)

Hook: Appropriate size hook to achieve a firm gauge with selected yarn

2 stitch markers

Tapestry needle

SPECIAL ABBREVIATIONS
Hdc2tog: Half double crochet 2 stitches together

Sl st-picot: Ch 3, sl st in base of chain.

INSTRUCTIONS

Flower

Row 1: Using A, ch 6, (sl st-picot) 3 times, working back across ch, sl st, 5 sc. Ch 2, rotate work so you are looking at the base of the original ch. Working in free lps of the original ch, 4 sc, ch 14, PM in 4th ch from hook, turn.

Row 2: Beg in 3rd ch from hook, (sc2tog) 6 times, working along the sc, 4 sc, (2 sc, ch 2, sc) in ch-2 sp, rotate work, 4 sc, ch 14, PM in the 4th ch from hook, turn.

Row 3: Beg in 3rd ch from hook, (sc2tog) 6 times, working along the sc, 5 sc, sc in ch-2 sp, ch 5, sc in 3rd ch from hook, working along ch, 2 sc, sc in ch-2 sp. Working up the other side of the piece, 2 sc, ch 5, curl the top petal around and sl st in marked st, remove marker, ch 14, PM in the 5th ch from hook, turn.

Row 4: Beg in 3rd ch from hook, (sc2tog) 6 times, sc in sl st. Continuing along ch, sc, sc2tog, 2 sc. Working along the sc, 6 sc, (2 sc, ch 2, sc) in ch-2 sp, rotate piece to work up the other side, 6 sc, ch 5, curl the top petal around and sl st in marked st, remove marker, ch 14, PM in the 5th ch from hook, turn.

Row 5: Beg in 3rd ch from hook, (sc2tog) 6 times, sc in sl st. Continuing along ch, sc, sc2tog, 2 sc. Working along the sc, 7 sc, sc in ch-2 sp, ch 5, sc in 3rd ch from hook, working along ch, 2 sc, sc in ch-2 sp. Working up the other side of the piece, 3

sc, ch 6, curl previous petal around and sl st in marked st, remove marker, ch 26, PM in 4th ch from hook, turn.

Row 6: Beg in 3rd ch from hook, (sc2tog) 12 times, sc in sl st. Continuing to work along ch, 2 sc, curl the long petal around and sl st in marked st, remove marker. Working along ch once again, sc2tog, 2 sc. Working along the sc, 7 sc, (2 sc, ch 2, sc) in ch-2 sp, rotate, 6 sc, ch 6, curl previous petal around and sl st in marked st, remove marker, ch 26, PM in 4th ch from hook, turn.

Row 7: Beg in 3rd ch from hook, (sc2tog) 12 times, sc in sl st. Continuing to work along ch, 2 sc, curl the long petal around and sl st in marked st, remove marker. Working along ch once again, sc2tog, 2 sc. Working along the sc, 7 sc, (sc, sl st) in ch-2 sp, fasten off.

Calyx

With B, ch 12.

Row 1: Sc in 3rd ch from hook, hdc, 2 dc, 2 hdc, 4 sc, rotate. Working in the unused loops along the other side of the ch, 7 sc, ch 4, turn.

Row 2: Sk 4 ch, 7 sc, sc in ch-2 sp, ch 2, rotate. Working along the other side of the piece, 7 sc, ch 4, turn.

Row 3: Sk 4 ch, 7 sc, (sc, sl st) in ch-2 sp.

If you want to add a stem, go on to the Stem instructions.

If you want to stop here, fasten off.

Stem (optional)

You'll make little leaves along the stem as you go.

*Ch 14.

To make a leaf, sl st in 4th ch from hook, (2 sc) in next st, (2 hdc) in next st.

Rep from * 3 times or just short of desired length of stem. Ch 10, turn.

Sc in 3rd ch from hook, 7 sc. This brings you opposite of a leaf.

**Ch 8, turn, sl st in 4th ch from hook, sc2tog, hdc2tog, sl st in st of the opposite leaf which already has 2-hdc in it.

Working up ch, 8 sc.

Rep from ** 3 times or to beg of stem, leaving a long tail for sewing, cut yarn and needle join to base of calyx.

Finishing

Sew calyx to base of flower. Weave in ends. Block, unfurling the petals and leaves.

Paisley

The paisley is a graceful motif that only gets better the more you embellish it! This crocheted version is fairly simple as far as paisleys go, but the picot border may remind you of more extravagant paisley possibilities.

INSTRUCTIONS

Both Paisleys

With A, ch 5, join with sl st in first ch to form a ring.

Rnd 1: Ch 5 (counts as dc and ch 2), (dc, ch 2) 4 times in ring, join with sl st in 3rd st of original ch to form a ring—5 dc spokes separated by ch-2.

Rnd 2: Ch 1, *sl st in next ch-2 sp, (5 dc) in next dc; rep from * 4 times, join with sl st in first st of rnd.

Rnd 3: Ch 1, working from the back, *sc around the post of the next dc of rnd 1, ch 4; rep from * 4 times, join with sl st to first sc of rnd. Fasten off.

MAKE LEAF

Join B with sl st in any sc of rnd 3, ch 10, sc in 5th ch from hook (you just created a 4-st turning lp), working along the ch, hdc, dc, htr, 2 tr, sl st in next sc of rnd 3. Continuing in the same direction, follow instructions for the left-curving or right-curving paisley.

Left-Curving Paisley

Left-Rnd 4: (Sc, ch 2, hdc, ch 2) in next ch-sp; *(dc, ch 2, dc, ch 2) in next ch-sp; rep from * once, (hdc, ch 2, hdc, ch 2) in next ch-sp.

Working up the side of the leaf in the free lps of the chain, sk first ch (it has a tr in it), hdc, ch 2, sk 2, hdc, ch 2, (hdc, ch 2, dc, ch 2, tr, ch 2, sc) all in turning lp. Working down the other side of the leaf, ch 2, sk 1 st, hdc, ch 2, sk 2, hdc, ch 2, sc in the top of the sc at the beg of rnd 4. Sl st in next ch-sp, fasten off B.

SKILL LEVEL
Intermediate

MATERIALS & TOOLS
4 colors of yarn of similar weight: flower color (A), leaf color (B), inner outline color (C), picot edging color (D)

Hook: Appropriate size hook to achieve a firm gauge with selected yarn

Tapestry needle

SPECIAL ABBREVIATIONS
Htr (half treble crochet): Yo 2 times, insert hook in stitch and draw up a loop (4 loops on hook), yo and draw through 2 loops (3 loops on hook), yo and draw through 3 loops (1 loop left on hook).

Sl st-picot: Ch 3, sl st in base of chain.

PATTERN NOTE
These instructions refer to left-curving and right-curving paisleys. If you crochet with the hook in your left hand, my left curve will be your right curve, and vice versa.

This pattern is written for 4 colors, but you can change colors less if you want to. If you're not going to change colors, and a round begins with hdc, you should ch 2 to replace that hdc; if the round begins with sc, ch 1 before you make the sc.

To hold a yarn double, pull the ends from the outside and inside of the skein or wind 2 small balls.

FOR THESE FLOWERS WE USED

Berroco Ultra® Alpaca (50% super fine alpaca, 50% Peruvian wool; 3.5oz/100g = 215yd/198m): (A) color orange #6263; (B) color green #6262; (C) color heathery green #6273; (D) color violet #6219— light weight yarn; (3)

GAUGE CIRCLE
(see page 11) = 1"/2.5cm worked on 4.00mm (size G-6 U.S.) hook

FINISHED MEASUREMENTS
3"/7.6cm x 4¾/12cm

Cascade Yarns Kid Seta (held double) Cascade Kid Seta (70% kid mohair, 30% silk; 0.89oz/25g = 230yd/209m): held double, (A) color red #16; (B) color peach #14; (C) color cream #02; (D) color blue-green #25; (solid color flower) color taupe #13—superfine weight yarn; (1)

GAUGE CIRCLE
(see page 11) = ¾"/0.9cm worked on 3.50mm (size 00 steel U.S.) hook with yarn held double

FINISHED MEASUREMENTS
2¼"/5.7cm x 3⅝"/9.2cm

Left-Rnd 5: Join C with 4 sc in the same ch-sp, (4 sc in next ch-sp) 5 times, (3 sc in next ch-sp) 6 times, (sc, hdc, dc) all in tr at tip of paisley, ch 1, (2 sc in next ch-sp) twice, (3 sc in next ch-sp) twice, join with sl st to first sc of rnd. Fasten off C.

Left-Rnd 6: Join D with hdc in 2nd sc of rnd 5, (sl st-picot, sk 1, hdc in next st) 20 times, sl st-picot, hdc in next st, sl st-picot, dc in next st, sl st-picot, (tr, sl st-picot, tr, ch 1, 3 sl st-picots, sl st in the ch-1 just before

the picots, hdc) all in the dc at the tip of the paisley, sc in ch-st, (sk 1 st, hdc) twice, (ch 1, sk 1 st, hdc) 3 times, ch 1, cut yarn and needle join to first hdc of rnd.

Right-Curving Paisley
Right-Rnd 4: (Sc, ch 2, hdc, ch 2) in next ch-sp; *(dc, ch 2, dc, ch 2) in next ch-sp; rep from * once, (hdc, ch 2, hdc, ch 2) in next ch-sp.

Working up the side of the leaf in the free lps of the chain, sk first ch (it has a tr in it), hdc, ch 2, sk 1, hdc, ch 2, (sc, ch 2, tr, ch 2, dc, ch 2, hdc) all in the turning lp. Working down the other side of the leaf, ch 2, sk 2 st, hdc, ch 2, sk 1, hdc, ch 2, sc in the top of the sc at the beg of rnd 4. Sl st in next ch-sp, fasten off B.

Right-Rnd 5: Join C with 3 sc in the same ch-sp, (4 sc in next ch-sp) 6 times, (3 sc in next ch-sp) 2 times, (2 sc in next ch-sp) twice, ch 1, (dc, hdc, sc) all in tr at tip of paisley, (3 sc in next ch-sp) 5 times, join with sl st to first sc of rnd. Fasten off C.

Right-Rnd 6: Join D with hdc in 2nd sc of rnd 5, (sl st-picot, sk 1, hdc) 12 times, (ch 1, sk 1 st, hdc) 4 times, sk 1, hdc, sk 1, sc in the ch, (hdc, ch 1, 3 sl st-picots, sl st in the ch-1 just before the picots, tr, sl st-picot, tr) in the dc at the tip of the paisley, sl st-picot, dc in next st, (sl st-picot, hdc in next st) twice, (sl st-picot, sk 1, hdc) 7 times, sl st-picot, cut yarn and needle join to first hdc of rnd.

Finishing
Weave in ends, block.

Flamenco Key Fob

This bright key fob will be easy to find in the deep, dark recesses of your handbag. You might prefer to show it off by hanging it from the key loop on your backpack or purse.

SKILL LEVEL
Intermediate

FINISHED MEASUREMENTS
2¼"/5.7cm x 3¼"/8.3cm (flower only)

MATERIALS & TOOLS
Yummy Yarns Jelly Yarn Super Fine (100% vinyl; 1.35oz/38g = 60yd/55m): (A) color Pink Parfait; (B, C, D) color Black Licorice—light weight yarn;

Lotion or other lubricant for the hook (we used Burt's Bees® Hand Salve)

Crochet hook: 3.50mm (size E-4 U.S.) or size to obtain gauge

Strips of plastic cut from a plastic grocery bag, as needed

Tapestry needle

Key ring

GAUGE CIRCLE
(see page 11) = ⅝"/1.6cm worked on worked on 3.50mm (size E-4 U.S.) hook

INSTRUCTIONS

Crochet a Flamenco Flower (page 94), using colors as noted at left, and with the changes below.

To stuff the Shape Holder, use strips of plastic cut from a plastic grocery bag.

For the stem, ch 14, sc in 2nd ch from hook, sc in each rem ch, and attach as described in pattern. Cut yarn, leaving a long tail for sewing. Unfurl the stem, sew end to top of sepals to form a loop. Finish as described in Flamenco Flower pattern, making sure the sepals and stem are secure.

Finishing

Insert looped stem of Flamenco Flower onto key ring.

Daisy Coasters

Enjoy a delicious beverage while this thirsty cotton coaster protects your furniture. These bright colors remind me of summer and endless glasses of iced water. For steamy winter drinks, I might make these in richer, darker colors.

SKILL LEVEL
Intermediate

FINISHED MEASUREMENTS
5"/12.7cm across

MATERIALS & TOOLS
Lion Brand Lion® Cotton (100% cotton; 5oz/142g = 236yd/215m): (A) color Sunflower #157, (B) color White #100, (C) color Morning Glory Blue #108—medium weight yarn;

Crochet hook: 5.00mm (size H-8 U.S.) or size to obtain gauge

Washable craft felt or felted wool (ours is from The Wool Den, Lebanon, Ohio)

Washable fabric glue

Stiff paint brush for applying glue

Tapestry needle

Compass or circle template about 3¾"/9.6cm in diameter or the size you need to cover the bottom of the center of the flower.

Heavy book or other flat weight

Sewing thread and needle (optional)

GAUGE CIRCLE
(see page 11) = 1⁵⁄₁₆"/3.3cm worked on 5.00mm (size H-8 U.S.) hook

INSTRUCTIONS

For each coaster, crochet a large Russian Picot Daisy in colors of your choice or the ones listed above.

Use a compass or a circle template (I used the rim of a plastic drinking cup) to mark a circle on the felt, the correct size to cover the bottom of the flower center (rnds 1-4 or 1-5).

Cut out the felt circle.

Finishing

Brush fabric glue onto the felt and glue it to the bottom of the flower.

Place the glued flower on a flat surface and weigh it down with a heavy book or other flat weight. Let glue dry.

If desired, for more secure edges, whip stitch edge of felt to bottom of flower with sewing thread.

Fun and Fantastic Garden

Frost Flower

Thanks to the snowflake photography of Wilson Bentley and, more recently, Kenneth Libbrecht and others, we can study and marvel at the flower-like beauty of the water crystals we call snow.

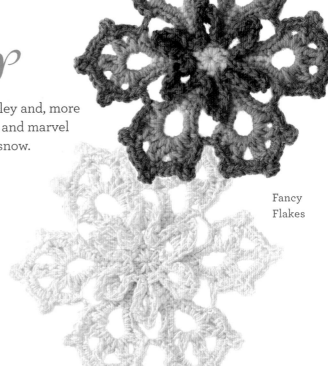

Fancy Flakes

INSTRUCTIONS

Basic Frost Flower

With A, ch 4, join with sl st in first ch to form a ring.

Rnd 1: Ch 1, *sc in ring, ch 15, sc in 11th ch from hook, 2 sc, ch 2; rep from * 5 times, join with sl st to first sc of rnd—6 petals.

Rnd 2: Working up the side of the next petal, sl st in each ch, then working in free lps of original ch, sl st, *2 sc, (3 sc, ch 2, 2 hdc-CL, ch 2, 2 dc-CL, ch 3, 2 tr-CL, ch 3, 2 dc-CL, ch 2, 2 hdc-CL, ch 2, 3 sc) all in large ch-sp at tip of petal; working down other side of petal, 2 sc, sl st, ch 2; moving

to the next petal, ‡ sk 2 ch, sl st in free lp at base of next sc; rep from * 4 times. Rep between * and ‡, sk the first 2 sl sts (which are in the ch of the first petal), sl st in next sl st and fasten off OR, for better results, cut yarn and needle join over first sl st.

Rnd 3: Counting from where you fastened off A, sk 5 sc and join A or B with sl st in next ch-2 sp, *sc in top of the 2 hdc-CL, (2 sc) in ch-2 sp, sc in the 2 dc-CL, hdc-picot, (4 sc) in ch-3 sp, (sc, hdc-picot, sc) in 2 tr-CL, (4 sc) in ch-3 sp, hdc-picot, sc in 2 dc-CL, (2 sc) in ch-2 sp, sc in top of 2 hdc-CL,

sl st in next ch-2 sp, ch 2, ‡ go to the next petal, sl st in ch-2 sp just before the next 2 hdc-CL; rep from * 4 times. Rep from * to ‡, then cut yarn and needle join to the first sl st of rnd.

Fancy Flake

Make the Basic Frost Flower, rnds 1-3 above. Note how the last 2 ch of a petal (rnd 1), the first 2 ch of the next petal, and the ch-2 sp between petals (rnd 2) form a small triangle near the center of the flower. You will crochet around those ch to make rnd 4.

SKILL LEVEL
Intermediate

MATERIALS & TOOLS
1 or 2 colors of yarn of similar weight: middle of the petal color (A), outer and inner petal color (B)

Hook: Appropriate size hook to achieve a firm gauge with selected yarn

Tapestry needle

SPECIAL ABBREVIATIONS
2 dc-CL: Yo, insert hook in next stitch, yo and draw up a loop, yo, draw through 2 loops on hook; yo, insert hook in next stitch, yo and draw up a loop, yo, draw through 2 loops on hook; yo, draw through all loops on hook, ch 1 to close the CL.

2 hdc-CL: Yo, insert hook in next stitch, yo and draw up a loop, yo, insert hook in next stitch, yo and draw up a loop, yo and draw through all loops on hook, ch 1 to close the CL.

2 tr-CL: (Yo) twice, insert hook in next stitch, yo and draw up a loop, (yo, draw through 2 loops on hook) twice; (yo) twice, insert hook in next stitch, yo and draw up a loop, (yo, draw through 2 loops on hook) twice; yo, draw through all loops on hook, ch 1 to close the CL.

Hdc-picot: Ch 3, hdc in base of chain.

Sl st-picot: Ch 3, sl st in base of chain.

PATTERN NOTE
The symbol ‡ is a marker in the pattern. Ignore it until the instructions tell you otherwise. The optional round 4 adds texture to the Basic Frost Flower.

The pattern is written for one or two colors, but you can change color for every round.

FOR THESE FLOWERS WE USED
Berroco Ultra® Alpaca (50% super fine alpaca, 50% Peruvian wool; 3.5oz/100g = 215yd/198m): (Rnd 1) color yellow #6225; (Rnd 2) color green #6262; (Rnd 3) color heathery green #6273; (Rnd 4) color purple #62171—light weight yarn; **(3)**

GAUGE CIRCLE
(see page 11) = 1"/2.5cm worked on 4.00mm (size G-6 U.S.) hook

FINISHED MEASUREMENTS
6½"/16.5cm

Lion Brand LB Collection Silk Mohair (70% super kid mohair, 30% silk; 0.88oz/25g = 231yd/212m): (A) color Wisp #100; (B) color Sky Blue #106—superfine weight yarn; **(1)**

GAUGE CIRCLE
(see page 11) = ¾"/0.9cm worked on 3.50mm (size 00 steel U.S.) hook with yarn held double

FINISHED MEASUREMENTS
4½"/11.3cm

Berroco Seduce® (47% rayon, 25% linen, 17% silk, 11% nylon; 1.41oz/40g = 100yd/92m): (all rnds) color white Satin #4400—fine weight yarn; **(2)**

GAUGE CIRCLE
(see page 11) = ¾"/1.9cm worked on 3.50mm (size E-4 U.S.) hook

FINISHED MEASUREMENTS
5⅜"/13.6cm

Rnd 4: Find last 2 ch of a petal near the center of the flower. Fold the petal so you can work around that ch-2 sp. Join B or A with *(2 sc, hdc) in ch-2 sp, rotate the flower so you can see the ch-2 sp between the petals, (2 dc, sl st picot, 2 dc) in this ch-2 sp, rotate the flower again to see the ch-2 sp at the base of the next petal, (hdc, 2 sc) in this ch-2 sp. Rotate again to work in the ch-2 sp at the other side of the base of this petal. Rep from * 5 times, cut yarn and needle join to first sc of rnd.

Finishing
Weave in ends. Block the outer petals, pinning down each picot for best results. Block the center gently, so as not to squash it.

Basic
Frost Flower

Grandma's Windmill Flowers

Here's a trimmed-down and updated version of the old Windmill Pattern that has graced so many crocheted bedspreads. It's much easier than it looks.

SKILL LEVEL
Easy

MATERIALS & TOOLS
4 colors of yarn of similar weight: center color (A), inner petal color (B), middle petal color (C), outer petal color (D)

Hook: Appropriate size hook to achieve a firm gauge with selected yarn

Tapestry needle

SPECIAL ABBREVIATION
3 dc-CL: (yo, insert hook in indicated st, yo, draw up a lp, yo, draw through 2 lps on hook) 3 times, yo, draw through all lps on hook, ch 1 to close the CL.

FOR THESE FLOWERS WE USED
Berroco Ultra® Alpaca (50% super fine alpaca, 50% Peruvian wool; 3.5oz/100g = 215yd/198m): (A) color red #6234; (B) color taupe #6214; (C) color teal #6285; (D) color purple #62171—light weight yarn;

> **GAUGE CIRCLE**
> (see page 11) = 1"/2.5cm worked on 4.00mm (size G-6 U.S.) hook
>
> **FINISHED MEASUREMENTS**
> 4"/10cm

Dale of Norway Falk (100% superwash wool; 1¾oz/50g = 116yd/106m): (A) color Dandelion #2417; (B) color Off White #0017; (C) color Aquamarine #6604; (D) color Cerulean #6215—light weight yarn;

> **GAUGE CIRCLE**
> (see page 11) = 1"/2.5cm worked on 4.00mm (size G-6 U.S.) hook
>
> **FINISHED MEASUREMENTS**
> 3¾"/9.5cm

Cascade Pima Tencel (50% Peruvian cotton, 50% tencel; 1.75oz/50g = 109yd/99m): (A and C) color yellow #0258; (B) color white #0157; (D) color orange #3183—light weight yarn;

> **GAUGE CIRCLE**
> (see page 11) = 15⁄16"/2.4cm worked on 4.00mm (size G-6 U.S.) hook
>
> **FINISHED MEASUREMENTS**
> 4"/10cm

INSTRUCTIONS

Flower

With A, ch 9, join with sl st in first ch to form a ring.

Rnd 1: Ch 2, (yo, insert hook in ring, yo and draw up a lp, yo and draw through 2 lps on hook) twice, yo and draw through all lps on hook (this counts as the first 3 dc-CL), ch 3, *3 dc-CL in ring, ch 3; rep from * 7 times, join with sl st to top of ch-3 at beg of rnd. Fasten off A—nine 3 dc-CL separated by ch-3 lps.

Rnd 2: Join B. *(Sc, hdc, dc, ch 2, dc, hdc, sc) in next ch-3 lp, ch 2; rep from * 8 times, join with sl st to first sc of rnd. Fasten off B—9 petals.

Rnd 3: Join C. Beg in first sc of next petal, *3 sc, (sc, ch 2, sc) in ch-2 sp, 3 sc, ch 3; rep from * 8 times, join with sl st to first sc of rnd. Fasten off C.

Rnd 4: Join D. Beg in first sc of next petal, *3 sc, hdc, (hdc, ch 2, hdc) in ch-2 sp, hdc, 3 sc, ch 4; rep from * 8 times, join with sl st to first sc of rnd.

Rnd 5: Ch 4, turn so you are looking at the back side of the flower. This ch-4 is attached to the last sl st of the first petal. Now sl st in last sc of next petal. This pulls the previous petal behind this petal and anchors it there. Ch 4, (sl st in last sc of next petal, ch 4) 7 times, sl st in first st of rnd. Fasten off D—9 petals that overlap each other.

Finishing

Make sure all petals are arranged with one side under the previous petal and one side over the next petal. Weave in ends. Block gently. For sharply pointed petals, pull out and pin the points before blocking.

Twirl Center Rose

This lovely and simple rose developed from my early failed attempts at making a shrimp flower. I snatched a rose from the jaws of a shrimp.

SKILL LEVEL
Easy

MATERIALS & TOOLS
1 yarn: flower color (A)

Hook: Appropriate size hook to achieve a firm gauge with selected yarn

Tapestry needle

PATTERN NOTE
In row 2, you will link the twirl to one of the petals. As you're working this row, you'll see the back side of the twirl. Insert your hook just below the front loop of the marked stitch, as you are looking at it. Later, when you turn the flower to look at its right side, the tops of the twirl stitches will swirl unbroken, because the join is behind them.

FOR THESE FLOWERS WE USED

Berroco Ultra® Alpaca (50% super fine alpaca, 50% Peruvian wool; 3.5oz/100g = 215yd/198m): (A) color purple #62171; (B) color orange #6263 or red #6236; (C) color yellow #6225; (D) color green #6273—light weight yarn; **(3)**

> **GAUGE CIRCLE**
> (see page 11) = 1"/2.5cm worked on 4.00mm (size G-6 U.S.) hook

> **FINISHED MEASUREMENTS**
> 2¾"/7cm x 3½"/9cm (single); 2¾"/7cm x 4¼"/11cm (double)

Ivy Brambles SockScene (100% superwash merino; 4oz/113g = 410yd/378m): (A) color Sunrise #008—superfine weight yarn; **(1)**

> **GAUGE CIRCLE**
> (see page 11) = ¾"/1.9cm worked on 3.25mm (size 0 steel U.S.) hook

> **FINISHED MEASUREMENTS**
> 1⅝"/4cm

Spud and Chloë Sweater (55% superwash wool, 45% organic cotton; 3.5oz/100g = 160yd/146m): (A) colors Jelly Bean #7513; Watermelon #7512; and Firefly #7505—medium weight yarn; **(4)**

> **GAUGE CIRCLE**
> (see page 11) = 1¼"/3cm worked on 5.00mm (size H-8 U.S.) hook

> **FINISHED MEASUREMENT**
> 2¾"/7cm

Berroco Ultra® Alpaca Light (50% super fine alpaca, 50% Peruvian wool; 1.75oz/50g = 144yd/133m): (A) color rose #4233—sport weight yarn; **(2)**

> **GAUGE CIRCLE**
> (see page 11) = ⅞"/2.1cm worked on 3.50mm (size E-4 U.S.) hook

> **FINISHED MEASUREMENTS**
> 1⅞"/4.6cm

INSTRUCTIONS

Flower

With A, ch 13.

Row 1: Sk 1 ch, (3 sc) in each of next 3 ch, PM in the last sc, (3 hdc) in each of next 3 ch, PM in the 4th hdc, (3 dc) in each of next 6 ch—36 sts. Ch 1, turn. Remember this ch, because you will join to it at the end of rnd 2.

Row 2: Work in FL only across this row. (Sl st, ch 2, dc) in the first st, (2 dc) in next st, (dc, ch 2, sl st) in next st.

*(Sl st, ch 2, dc) in next st, (2 dc) in next st, (dc, ch 2, sl st) in next st; rep from * once.

(Sl st, ch 2, dc) in next st, (2 dc) in next st, dc, ch 2, insert hook in same st as last dc, insert hook in the lp just below the front lp of the first marked st of row 1 (which is a sc), yo and complete sl st by pulling through all lps on hook—join complete. Remove marker.

Last petal: (Sl st, ch 2, dc) in next st, (2 dc) in next st, (dc, ch 2, sl st) in next st.

Sl st in the turning ch at base of the very first petal (you noted this st at the end of row 1). Fasten off.

Finishing

Weave in ends, block very gently. If you feel the twirly center needs to be more firmly attached, stitch in it from the back with tapestry needle as you weave in ends.

Paleo Plant & Pinecone

Cycads grew on this earth long before flowering plants, and they're still around today. They aren't related to pines, except for how easily you can turn the cycad stem into a pinecone.

SKILL LEVEL
Intermediate

MATERIALS & TOOLS
3 colors of yarn of similar weight: cycad stem or pinecone color (A), cycad top color (B), cycad base color (C)

Hook: Appropriate size hook to achieve a firm gauge with selected yarn

Marker, optional

Stuffing

Tapestry needle

SPECIAL ABBREVIATIONS
Hdc2tog: Half double crochet 2 stitches together

Htr (half treble crochet): Yo 2 times, insert hook in stitch and draw up a loop (4 loops on hook), yo and draw through 2 loops (3 loops on hook), yo and draw through 3 loops (1 loop left on hook).

FOR THESE FLOWERS WE USED

Cascade Yarns Jewel Hand Dyed (100% wool; 3.5oz/100g = 142yd/129m): (A) color gold #9284; (B) color pink #9283; (C) color green #9894—medium weight yarn; (■4■)

GAUGE CIRCLE
(see page 11) = 1⅜"/3.5cm worked on 6.00mm (size J-10 U.S.) hook

FINISHED MEASUREMENTS
(Paleo Plant) 6"/15.2cm (across the base) x 5"/12.8cm

Universal Yarns Fibra Natura Exquisite Bamboo (77% bamboo, 23% superwash merino wool; 1.76oz/50g = 109yd/100m): (A) color Sable #40156—medium weight yarn; (■4■)

GAUGE CIRCLE
(see page 11) = ⅞"/2.2cm worked on 4.00mm (size G-6 U.S.) hook

FINISHED MEASUREMENTS
(Pinecone) 2⅜"/5.9cm x 3"/7.5cm

INSTRUCTIONS

Cycad Stem

With A, ch 4, join with sl st in first ch to form a ring. This is the central chain ring. This section is worked in a continuous spiral; do not join at ends of rnds, but mark ends if desired to help you keep track of st counts.

Rnd 1: Ch 2 (counts as first hdc), 11 hdc in ring—12 hdc.

Rnd 2: Working in BL, (2 sc) in 2nd ch of rnd 1, sc, (2 sc) in next st, *(2 sc) in next st, sc, (2 sc) in next st; rep from * twice—20 sc.

Rnd 3: Working in BL, *2 hdc, (2 hdc) in next st, 2 hdc; rep from * 3 times—24 hdc.

Rnd 4: Working in BL, 24 hdc.

Rnd 5: Working in BL, *4 hdc, hdc2tog; rep from * 3 times—20 hdc.

Rnd 6: Working in BL, *2 hdc, hdc2tog, hdc; rep from * 3 times—16 hdc.

Rnd 7: Working in BL, *hdc2tog, 2 hdc; rep from * 3 times—12 hdc.

Rnd 8: Working in BL, *hdc, hdc2tog; rep from * 3 times—8 hdc. Stuff the piece lightly.

Rnd 9: Working in BL, (hdc2tog) 3 times, some sts remain unworked. Stuff a little more, if needed. Ch 1, turn.

Pinecone

Cycad

The FL of the sts form a line spiraling around the cone. Work in those sts for the next rnd.

Rnd 10: Working in FL of the previous sts, sk ch, sl st in next st, sk 1, (5 dc) in next st, *sk 1 st, sl st, sk 1 st, (5 dc) in next st; rep from * around and around the cone, until about 5 sts rem. Fasten off, leaving a long tail for sewing.

Cycad Top

With B, ch 4, join with sl st in first ch to form a ring.

Rnd 1: Ch 1, *sc in ring, (ch 6, working back along ch, sk 1 ch, 3 sl st, and 2 ch rem unworked for stem) 2 times, (ch 4, working back along chs, sk 1 ch, 3 sl st) twice. Sl st in each of the next 2 stem sts, ch 4, working back along chs, sk 1 ch, 3 sl st, sl st in each of rem 2 stem sts; rep from * 4 times, join with sl st to the first sc of rnd.

Rnd 2: Fold fronds to the back, (sl st in next sc) 5 times. Leaving a long tail for sewing, cut yarn and needle join to first st of rnd.

Cycad Base

With C, ch 6, join with sl st in first ch to form a ring.

Rnd 1 (RS): Ch 4 (counts as first tr), 17 tr in ring, join with sl st to 4th ch of rnd—18 tr.

Rnd 2: Ch 1, *2 sc, (2 sc) in next st; rep from * 5 times. Join with sl st to the first sc of rnd—24 sc.

Rnd 3: Ch 1, *sc in next st, ch 15, sl st in 3rd ch from hook, working back along ch, 2 sc, 2 hdc, 2 dc, 2 htr, 4 tr, sk 2 sts of rnd 1; rep from * 7 times. Join with sl st in first sc of rnd.

Rnd 4 (WS): Turn the flower over so you are looking at the WS. *Ch 3, looking at the next petal, sk 4 tr and htr, sl st around post of next st, ch 3, sl st in st between this petal and the next petal; rep from * 5 times, join with sl st to first sc of rnd. Fasten off.

Cycad Finishing

Block the Cycad Top only.

*Weave a length of yarn up the center on the WS of a frond to just short of its tip. Shape the frond so it arches a little bit, then weave the yarn back to the base of the frond. Rep from * 4 times, changing yarn when necessary. Tack to hold yarn in place, trim yarn. This keeps the fronds from drooping.

Sew the flat end of the Cycad Stem to the center of the right side of the Cycad Base. Sew the center of the Cycad Top to the tip of the Cycad Stem. Weave in ends.

Pinecone

Make the Cycad Stem through rnd 10, but do not fasten off. The rem sts are the sts of rnd 1. Insert hook between next 2 sts of rnd 1, and allow the hook to come out from the central chain ring. Yo and complete a sl st. Ch 6, hdc in 2nd ch from hook, 4 sc. Insert hook in central chain ring, sk 3 sts of rnd 1, and allow the hook to come out between the next 2 sts of Rnd 1. Yo and complete a sl st. Fasten off.

Pinecone Finishing

Weave in ends. Do not block.

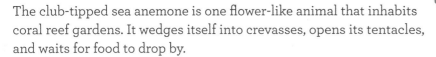

Anemone & Friend

The club-tipped sea anemone is one flower-like animal that inhabits coral reef gardens. It wedges itself into crevasses, opens its tentacles, and waits for food to drop by.

Large Anemone

SKILL LEVEL
Intermediate

MATERIALS & TOOLS
1-3 colors of yarn of similar weight: center color (A), frill color (B), petal color (C)

Hook: Appropriate size hook to achieve a firm gauge with selected yarn

Tapestry needle

SPECIAL ABBREVIATIONS
2 dc-CL: Yo, insert hook in next stitch, yo and draw up a loop, yo, draw through 2 loops on hook; yo, insert hook in same stitch, yo and draw up a loop, yo, draw through 2 loops on hook; yo, draw through all 3 loops on hook, ch 1 to close the CL.

Sl st-picot: Ch 3, sl st in base of chain.

INSTRUCTIONS

Large Anemone

Rnd 1: With A, (sl st-picot) 6 times, join with sl st in the loop at the base of the first picot to form a ring—6 picots in a ring.

Rnd 2: Looking at RS of the picots (they will be upside down), ch 1, sc in the same lp as the sl st, (sc in the lp at the base of the next picot) 5 times, join with sl st to first sc of rnd—6 sc.

Rnd 3: Ch 1, *2 sc, (2 sc) in next st; rep from * once, join with sl st to first sc of rnd—8 sc.

Rnd 4: Ch 1, *sc, (2 sc) in next st, 2 sc; rep from * once, join with sl st to first sc of rnd—10 sc.

Rnd 5: Ch 1, *sc, (2 sc) in next st; rep from * 4 times, join with sl st to first sc of rnd—15 sc.

Rnd 6: Ch 1, [(2 sc) in next st, sc] 3 times, sc, [(2 sc) in next st, sc] 3 times, 2 sc, join with sl st to first sc of rnd—21 sc.

Rnd 7: Ch 1, [sc, (2 sc) in next st] 3 times, 4 sc, [sc, (2 sc) in next st] 3 times, 4 sc, (2 sc) in next st, join with sl st to first sc of rnd—28 sc. Fasten off A.

Rnd 8: Join B with sc in FL of any st of rnd 7, *ch 4, sk 1 st, sc in FL of next st; rep from * 12 times, ch 4, cut yarn and needle join to first sc of rnd.

Rnd 9: Working in BL of rnd 5, join C with *sl st in next st, ch 8, (2 dc-CL, ch 2, sl st) in 3rd ch from hook. Working down the ch, sl st, sc, 3 hdc, sk 1 st of rnd 5; rep from * 13 times, sl st in next st of rnd 5 (there is already a st there)—14 tentacles, or petals, if you prefer. Fasten off if desired, or for a more extravagant look, add more petals in rnd 10.

Rnd 10: Ch 1. Continue to work in the BL of rnd 5, in the skipped sts of last rnd. Fold the petals of rnd 7 forward, out of the way. *Sl st in next skipped st, ch 10, (2 dc-CL, ch 2, sl st) all in 3rd ch from hook. Working down the ch, sl st, sc, 5 hdc; rep from * 13 times, sl st in the first st of this rnd. Fasten off—14 petals.

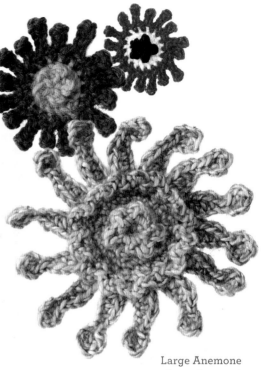

Small Anemones

FOR THESE FLOWERS WE USED

Berroco Ultra® Alpaca (50% super fine alpaca, 50% Peruvian wool; 3.5oz/100g = 215yd/198m): (A) color green #6262; (B) color teal #6285; (C) color violet #6219—light weight yarn; (3)

GAUGE CIRCLE
(see page 11) = 1"/2.5cm worked on 4.00mm (size G-6 U.S.) hook

FINISHED MEASUREMENTS
5⅜"/13.2cm (large anemone); 3"/7.5cm (small anemone)

Prism Indulgence (68% silk, 15% wool, 12% kid mohair, 5% nylon; 2oz/56g = 92yd/84m): (A, B, and C) color Mojave—medium weight yarn; (4)

GAUGE CIRCLE
(see page 11) = 1⅛"/2.9cm worked on 5.00mm (size H-8 U.S.) hook

FINISHED MEASUREMENTS
5¾"/14.5cm (single rnd of petals)

Coats & Clark Aunt Lydia's Classic Crochet Thread, No. 10, Art. 154, (100% mercerized cotton, 350yd/320m (colors), 400yd/364m (white)): (A) color White #0001; (B) colors Pagoda Red #0901; (Small Anemone Center) color Black #0012—10-count crochet thread; (0)

GAUGE CIRCLE
(see page 11) = ⅜"/0.9cm worked on 2.00mm (size 4 steel U.S.) hook

FINISHED MEASUREMENTS
1⅝"/4cm

Large Anemone
Through Round 9

Small Anemone

With A, ch 5, join with sl st in first ch to form a ring.

Rnd 1: Ch 3 (counts as first dc), 15 dc in ring, join with sl st to 3rd ch of rnd. Fasten off A—16 dc.

Rnd 2: Join B with *sc in next st of rnd 1, ch 4, hdc in 2nd ch from hook, working down ch, 2 sl st, sc in next st of rnd 1, ch 5, hdc in 2nd ch from hook, working down ch, 3 sl st; rep from * 7 times, cut yarn and needle join to first sc of rnd.

SMALL ANEMONE CENTER

With A or color of choice, (sl st-picot) 5 times. Fasten off, leaving a long tail for sewing. Thread tail on tapestry needle, arrange the picots in a ring. Look at the right side of the picots. insert the needle from underneath to top of the very first ch, then slip the needle underneath the loop that sits on top edge of each picot. It is the front loop of the sl st that you used to form the picot. You'll end with 6 loops on the tapestry needle.

Pull the tail to close the center of the picot ring. Take the needle under the first chain one more time, and then take it down the center of the tiny flower. Tighten if necessary, tack to secure.

Use the remaining tail to sew the Center piece to the top of the Small Anemone.

Finishing

Weave in ends. If you like the sea-anemone look, don't block the Large Anemone. The petals will curl forward and look more like tentacles. For a more flowery look, steam the Large Anemone gently, stretching out the petals and pinning if necessary to keep them flat. Don't squash the 3-dimensional center. After weaving in ends, block the Small Anemone, stretching out its petals and pinning if necessary to keep them from curling.

Rafflesita

Rafflesia arnoldii is the biggest flower in the world, measuring about 3 feet (1m) across. It grows in the rain forests of Indonesia. This little crocheted version, with its diminutive name, smells a lot nicer than the original.

SKILL LEVEL
Intermediate

MATERIALS & TOOLS
1 or more colors of yarn as desired; pattern is written for variegated yarn: flower color (A)

Hook: Appropriate size hook to achieve a firm gauge with selected yarn

Embroidery floss, beads, or buttons to decorate center of flower.

Tapestry needle

PATTERN NOTE
Try changing color for each round, mixing variegated yarns with matching solids.

INSTRUCTIONS

Flower

With A, ch 4, join with sl st in first ch to form a ring.

Rnd 1: Ch 3 (counts as first dc), 11 dc in ring, join with sl st in 3rd ch of rnd—12 dc.

Rnd 2: Ch 3 (counts as first dc), dc in same st as sl st, (2 dc) in each st around, join with sl st in FL of the 3rd ch of rnd—24 dc.

Rnd 3: Ch 1, working in FL only, sc in each st around, join with sl st in first sc of rnd. This rnd won't be seen in the finished flower. It is used to support rnd 7—24 sc.

Rnd 4: Ch 1, working in BL of rnd 2, *3 sc, (2 sc) in next st; rep from * 5 times, join with sl st to first sc of rnd—30 sc.

Rnd 5 (Petal Rnd): Each petal is worked in 7 mini-rows, which are joined with sl sts to the back loops of rnd 4.

5A: *Ch 6, working down ch toward the base of the petal, hdc in 3rd ch from hook, 2 dc, sc, sl st in BL of next st of rnd 4, ch 1, turn.

FOR THESE FLOWERS WE USED

Lion Brand Sock-Ease™ (75% wool, 25% nylon; 3.5oz/100g = 438yd/400m): (A) color Lemon Drop #204— super fine weight yarn; (**1**)

GAUGE CIRCLE
(see page 11) = ¹¹⁄₁₆"/1.7cm worked on 3.25mm (size 0 steel U.S.) hook

FINISHED MEASUREMENTS
3⅜"/8.5cm

Brooks Farm Yarns Duet (55% kid mohair, 45% fine wool; 8oz/225g = 500yd/455m): (A) color shaded red/gold—light weight yarn; (**3**)

Dragonfly button #92191 by JHB

GAUGE CIRCLE
(see page 11) = ⅞"/2.2cm worked on 4.00mm (size G-6 U.S.) hook

FINISHED MEASUREMENTS
4¾"/12cm

Judi & Co. Cordé (100% rayon with a cotton core, 144 yd/132m) (A) color Cherry BonBon—bulky weight yarn; (**4**)

GAUGE CIRCLE
(see page 11) = 1⅛"/2.8cm worked on 5.00mm (size H-8 U.S.) hook

FINISHED MEASUREMENTS
6"/15.2cm

5B: Working toward outer edge of petal, sk the ch and the sl st, sc, dc, (2 dc) in next st, dc, dc in top of turning ch, ch 3, turn.

5C: Working toward base of petal, 4 dc, sc, sk 1 st of rnd 4, sl st in BL of next st of rnd 4, ch 1, turn.

5D: Working toward outer edge of petal, sk the ch and the sl st, sc, 4 dc, dc in turning ch, ch 3, turn.

5E: Working toward base of petal, 4 dc, sc, sk 1 st of rnd 4, sl st in BL of next st of rnd 4, ch 1, turn.

5F: Working toward outer edge of petal, sk the ch and the sl st, sc, dc, dc2tog, dc, dc in top st of turning ch, ch 2, turn.

5G: Working toward base of petal, hdc, 2 dc, sc, sl st in BL of next st of rnd 4.

Rep from * 4 times.

Rnd 6 (Petal Outline Rnd): You will sl st around each petal. Take care to insert hook in the very edge lps (NOT under a turning ch or dc). *Working in the free lps up the side of the next petal, sl st in each st. Working across the top of the petal, 16 sl sts spaced evenly across the top. This works out to about one st in each turning ch, and 2 or 3 sts in the side lps of each dc. Working down the other side of the petal, sl st in each st, sl st in st between petals. Rep from * 4 times. Do the best you can. Examine each petal before moving on to the next one. If it doesn't look good, take it out and do it again. Fasten off.

Rnd 7 (Ring Around the Center Rnd): Looking at RS of the flower center, find the free front loops of rnd 4. To work this rnd in the opposite direction of all the other rnds, hold the flower with the petal facing you and the flower center facing away from you. Beg with a dc in any FL of rnd 4, inserting hook under the loop from the petal side toward the center. Complete first dc. (Dc2tog, dc) 9 times, dc2tog, cut yarn and needle join to first dc of rnd.

Finishing

Weave in ends. Decorate the center of the flower with embroidery, beads, or an insect button. A fly button would be most realistic.

Candy Cornflower

As a kid, I loved candy corn, an overly-sweet Halloween treat. You could use the candies to make excellent false teeth and fangs, and if you arranged them in a ring, they looked like a very cute flower.

INSTRUCTIONS

Candy Cornflower

With A, ch 4, join with sl st in first ch to form a ring.

Rnd 1: Ch 2 (counts as first hdc), ch 2, (hdc in ring, ch 2) 6 times. Join with sl st to 2nd ch of rnd. Fasten off A.

Rnd 2: With B, (6 hdc in next ch-2 sp, popcorn-join this group of sts, ch 2) 7 times, join with sl st to first hdc of rnd. Fasten off B.

Rnd 3: Join C. *Sk first hdc of petal, (2 hdc) in each of the next 4 sts, popcorn-join this group of sts, ch 2, sl st in ch-2 lp between petals of rnd 1, ch 2, move to next petal; rep from * 6 times, join with sl st to first hdc of rnd.

Baby
Cornflowers

SKILL LEVEL
Intermediate

MATERIALS & TOOLS
3 or 4 colors of yarn of similar weight: yellow or center color (A), white or inside petal color (B), orange or middle petal color (C), and yellow or outer petal color (D)

Hook: Appropriate size hook to achieve a firm gauge with selected yarn

Tapestry needle

SPECIAL ABBREVIATIONS
Hdc2tog: Half double crochet 2 stitches together

Popcorn-join: Remove hook from the last stitch, insert hook in the top of the first stitch of the group, reinsert hook in the open loop, pull the loop through the other loops on hook. Join complete.

PATTERN NOTE
When working in rounds with popcorn-joins, turn the flower as needed to work in the first few and last few stitches of each petal.

The Baby Cornflower looks nice from the front, where you see sturdy little popcorn petals, and from the back, where the petals form loops.

Candy
Cornflower

Baby
Cornflower

FOR THESE FLOWERS WE USED

Dale of Norway Falk (100% superwash wool; 1 3/4oz/50g = 116yd/106m): (A and D) color Dandelion #2417; (B) color Off White #0017; (C) color Orange #3418—light weight yarn; (3)

GAUGE CIRCLE
(see page 11) = 1"/2.5cm worked on 4.00mm (size G-6 U.S.) hook

FINISHED MEASUREMENTS
(Candy Cornflower) 3½"/9cm

Dale of Norway Baby Ull (100% merino wool; 1 ¾oz/50g = 180yd/165m): (A and D) color Yellow #2106, (B) color White #0010, (C) color Tangerine #2817—superfine weight yarn; (1)

GAUGE CIRCLE
(see page 11) = ¾"/1.9cm worked on 3.50mm (size E-4 U.S.) hook

FINISHED MEASUREMENTS
(Candy Cornflower) 2¾"/6.9cm;(Baby Cornflower) 1⅜"/3.4cm

If you prefer blue cornflowers, try Berroco Ultra® Alpaca (50% super fine alpaca, 50% Peruvian wool; 3.5oz/100g = 215yd/198m): (A) yellow #6225, (B) colors light blue #6239 and royal blue #6260—light weight yarn; (3)

GAUGE CIRCLE
(see page 11) = 1"/2.5cm worked on 4.00mm (size G-6 U.S.) hook

FINISHED MEASUREMENTS
1¾ to 2"/4.5 to 5cm

Rnd 4: Ch 2 (counts as first hdc), hdc, (2 hdc) in next st, 2 hdc, (2 hdc) in next st, 2 hdc, popcorn-join this group of sts, ch 6. *2 hdc, (2 hdc) in next st, 2 hdc, (2 hdc) in next st, 2 hdc, popcorn-join this group of sts, ch 6; rep from * 5 times, join with sl st to first hdc of rnd. Fasten off C.

Rnd 5: Join D with *hdc in first hdc of petal, hdc, (2 hdc) in next st, 4 hdc, (2 hdc) in next st, 2 hdc, popcorn-join this group of sts, ch 8, move to next petal; rep from * 6 times, join with sl st to first hdc of rnd.

Rnd 6: Sk 3 sts of petal, working in BL only, (hdc2tog) 3 times, sl st around ch between petals, ch 4, sl st around ch again, move to the next petal; rep from * 6 times, join with sl st to first st of rnd. This rnd bends to the back, forming the top of the candy corn motif.

Baby Cornflower
Work the instructions for the Candy Cornflower through rnd 2, except end by cutting thread and needle joining to first hdc of rnd.

Finishing
Weave in ends. Steam block the Candy Cornflower, straighten petals (they tend to torque a little when unblocked), pull them out to separate them, and make sure the last round folds nicely toward the back. Block the Baby Cornflowers.

Trillium & Fronds

These designs remind me of a meadow, where pretty flowers peek from among tall grasses. Varying the colors slightly, as I did here with reds and pinks, gives a natural look to your crocheted flower arrangements.

SKILL LEVEL
Easy

MATERIALS & TOOLS
3 colors of yarn of similar weight: flower center color (A), petal color (B), greenery color (C)

Hook: Appropriate size hook to achieve a firm gauge with selected yarn

Tapestry needle

SPECIAL ABBREVIATIONS
2 dc-CL: Yo, insert hook in next stitch, yo and draw up a loop, yo, draw through 2 loops on hook; yo, insert hook in same stitch, yo and draw up a loop, yo, draw through 2 loops on hook; yo, draw through all 3 loops on hook, ch 1 to close the CL.

Htr (half treble crochet): Yo 2 times, insert hook in stitch and draw up a loop (4 loops on hook), yo and draw through 2 loops (3 loops on hook), yo and draw through 3 loops (1 loop left on hook).

Sl st-picot: Ch 3, sl st in base of chain.

FOR THESE FLOWERS WE USED
Dale of Norway Falk (100% superwash wool; 1 3/4oz/50g = 116yd/106m): (A) colors Goldenrod #2427 and Dandelion #2417; (B) colors Poppy #3609, Red #4018, Pink #4415 Fuchsia #4516 and Magenta #4536; (C) colors Lime #8817, Fern #9155, and Spring Green #9133—light weight yarn; **3**

GAUGE CIRCLE
(see page 11) = 1"/2.5cm worked on 4.00mm (size G-6 U.S.) hook

FINISHED MEASUREMENTS
(Trillium) 3"/7.6cm; (Sawtooth Frond) 5/8"/1.5cm across, 5/8"/1.5cm per sawtooth lengthwise; (Scallop Frond) 3/8"/0.9cm across (single), 3/4"/2.8cm across (double), 5/8"/1.5cm per scallop lengthwise; (Paired Leaflet Frond) 1 5/8"/4cm across, 1 7/8"/4.9cm per repeat

INSTRUCTIONS

Flower

With A, ch 6, join with sl st in first ch to form a ring.

Rnd 1: *Ch 6, sc in 4th ch from hook (this forms a ch-3 sp), hdc, dc, sl st in ring (1 petal completed), ch 7, (2 dc-CL, ch 3, sl st) in 4th ch from hook, 3 sl sts (1 stamen completed), sl st in ring; rep from * twice, fasten off.

Rnd 2: With B, *working up the side of the next petal, placing sts in free lps of the ch, 2 sc, hdc, (2 dc, htr, sl st-picot, htr, 2 dc) in ch-3 sp at tip of petal. Working down other side of petal, hdc, 2 sc, sc in ring, fold the stamen toward the front of the work, sc in ring on the other side of the stamen. Rep from * twice, cut yarn and needle join to first sc of rnd.

Fronds

Use C for fronds.

Sawtooth Frond

Ch 39 or desired length of frond (multiple of 3 sts).

Row 1: *Ch 4, insert hook in 2nd ch from hook, yo and draw up a lp, (insert hook in next ch, yo and draw up the lp) twice (4 lps on hook). Yo and draw through all lps on hook. Sk 2 sts of ch, sl st in next ch; rep from * down the length of the ch. Fasten off.

Adjusting the curve: If you ch tightly, there will be a natural curve toward the ch. For a more pronounced curve toward the ch, sk only 1 ch between sawteeth. For a perfectly straight frond, make sure the original ch is loose, or skip more sts between saw-teeth.

Scallop Frond

Scallops all on one side: *Ch 5, dc in 5th ch from hook; rep from * until frond is desired length. Fasten off.

Scallops on both sides: *Ch 5, dc in 5th ch from hook; rep from * until frond is desired length. Working down the non-scallop side of the frond, **ch 4, sl st in next ch with a dc in it. Rep from ** down the length of the frond.

Paired Leaflet Frond

With C, ch 7, sc in 3rd ch from hook, 2 hdc, sc, sl st (top leaf).

*Ch 15 for stem. Sc in 3rd ch from hook, 2 hdc, (3 sc) in next st, ch 6, sc in 3rd ch

from hook, hdc2tog, sc, sl st in same st as the 3 sc. Rotate leaf pair so their tips are toward you, letting the yarn go behind your work as you rotate. With yarn behind work, sl st around the bottom edge of the leaf pair. Rep from * to just short of desired length, end with ch 9. Fasten off.

Finishing

Weave in ends. Block, pinning out the points of the trilliums, the length of the fronds, and the individual leaflets of the Paired Leaflet Frond.

Imp Flower

"A shrimp flower is supposed to curve," said my mom, trying to bend my little sample into the right shape. I liked its compact size, so I shortened the name to match the flower.

SKILL LEVEL
Easy

MATERIALS & TOOLS
3 colors of yarn of similar weight: flower color (A), bract or petal color (B), greenery color (C)

Hook: Appropriate size hook to achieve a firm gauge with selected yarn

Tapestry needle

SPECIAL ABBREVIATIONS
Htr (half treble crochet): Yo 2 times, insert hook in stitch and draw up a loop (4 loops on hook), yo and draw through 2 loops (3 loops on hook), yo and draw through 3 loops (1 loop left on hook).

Sl st-picot: Ch 3, sl st in base of chain.

PATTERN NOTE
To save time, crochet over the ends of A and B as you work down the chain.

If you want a longer flower, chain more stitches and increase the number of repeats in the color B.

FOR THESE FLOWERS WE USED

Cascade Pima Tencel (50% Peruvian cotton, 50% tencel; 1.75oz/50g = 109yd/99m): (A) color pale peach #9518; (B) color peach #9504; (C) color green #9500—light weight yarn; **(3)**

GAUGE CIRCLE
(see page 11) = ¹⁵⁄₁₆"/2.4cm worked on 4.00mm (size G-6 U.S.) hook

FINISHED MEASUREMENTS
1¾"/4.5cm x 3⅜"/8.5cm (including unblocked stem and flower)

Caron International Naturally Caron Country (25% merino wool, 75% microdenier acrylic; 3oz/85g = 185yd/170m): (A) color Naturally #0007; (B) color Spice House #0018; (C) color Loden Forest #0020—medium weight yarn; **(4)**

GAUGE CIRCLE
(see page 11) = 1"/2.5cm worked on 4.00mm (size G-6 U.S.) hook

FINISHED MEASUREMENTS
1½"/3.7cm x 3⅝"/9.2cm (including unblocked stem and flower)

INSTRUCTIONS

Flower

With A, ch 21, (sl st-picot) twice, sk picots, working down ch, 5 sc, sl st, fasten off A.

Join B in next ch with sl st, (ch 2, hdc, sl st-picot, hdc, ch 2, sl st) all in same st as sl st. [(Sl st, ch 2, hdc, sl st-picot, hdc, ch 2, sl st) all in next st] 5 times, [(sl st, ch 3, dc, sl st-picot, dc, ch 3, sl st) all in next st] 6 times, fasten off B.

To make the leaves, join C in next ch with sl st, (ch 4, htr, sl st-picot, htr, ch 4, sl st) all in same st as sl st, [(sl st, ch 4, htr, sl st-picot, htr, ch 4, sl st) all in next st] twice. Sl st in first st of C.

Stem: Ch 16, sc in 3rd ch from hook, sc 12. This brings you back to the base of the flower. Looking at the bottom of the leaf round, sl st between the next two leaves. Fasten off.

Finishing

Weave in ends. Weave one of the C ends around the base of the leaves, and one down the stem. Weave the A and B ends up the center of the flower. Do not block.

Flower Cloth Scarf

You can use any yarns that strike your fancy, make your favorite motifs, and customize the size of this scarf. And the best part? No gauge swatches necessary.

SKILL LEVEL
Varies depending on skill level of flowers used

FINISHED MEASUREMENTS
5"/12.5cm x 40"/112cm or desired size

MATERIALS & TOOLS
A collection of yarns in the same color family, plus one or two accent yarns. Yarns can be different weights and textures. (I used pink yarns, with caramel and cream accents.)

A variety of crochet hooks to give a firm gauge with your chosen yarns

Tapestry needle

Scrap fabric cut to the Finished Measurements or desired size (the fabric will not be part of the finished scarf)

Safety pins

Sewing thread and needle

GAUGE CIRCLE
Gauge is not required for this project.

INSTRUCTIONS

Read about Flower Cloth (page 16).

Make enough motifs to cover the fabric, including some very small motifs, such as Gauge Circles. Weave in the yarn ends and block. (I made several Paisleys, lots of Twirl Center Roses, and a dozen or so Gauge Circles (page 11) to fill gaps).

Place the motifs on the fabric, face down, arranging them to your satisfaction with as many edges touching as possible. Use small motifs to fill gaps.

Safety pin the motifs to the fabric.

Use sewing thread to sew together the motifs.

Unpin the scarf.

Flowery Shirts

The flowers on these shirts were arranged with the approval of a teenager.

SKILL LEVEL
Varies depending on skill level of flowers used

FINISHED MEASUREMENTS
Varies depending on size of shirt

MATERIALS & TOOLS

Purchased shirt or shirts, like the ones shown here from American Eagle

For gray and white shirt:

DMC Cebelia, No. 10 (100% mercerized cotton; (1.75oz/50g): (A and D) color Salmon #754; (B) color Mocha Cream #3033; (C) color Cream #712—10-count crochet thread; 🔟

For pink shirt:

Coats & Clark Aunt Lydia's Classic Crochet Thread, No. 10, Art. 154, (100% mercerized cotton, 350yd/320m): (A) color Goldenrod #0421; (B) color Hot Pink #0332; (C) color Aqua #0450—10-count crochet thread; 🔟

For both shirts:

Crochet hook: 2.00mm (size 4 steel U.S.) or size to obtain gauge

Tapestry needle

Safety pins or straight pins

Sewing thread and needle

GAUGE CIRCLE
For both threads, gauge circle (see page 11) = ½"/1.3cm worked on 2.00mm (size 4 steel U.S.) hook

INSTRUCTIONS

For the gray and white shirt, crochet two Paisleys, using the colors listed at left.

For the pink shirt, crochet five Trilliums, using the colors listed at left, and two lengths of Paired Leaf Frond. The length will vary with the shape and size of the neckline, so measure your Frond against the neckline of your shirt. Luckily the Paired Leaf Frond is easy to shorten or lengthen (as long as you don't cut the thread).

Arrange the motifs on the shirt and pin in place.

Sew around the edges, catching all the picots and corners.

Acknowledgments

Thanks first to all you crocheters who bought *Crochet Bouquet*. You made *Crochet Garden* possible! Thank you as well for your ideas for improvements or new patterns. I value every single comment and suggestion.

To my editor, Valerie Shrader, and the Needlearts Team at Lark Crafts: Thom, Meagan, Megan, Amanda, and the rest. Thank you for your guidance and your skill at turning a box full of samples and a bunch of words into a lovely book. You filled me with eager anticipation for the publication of *Crochet Garden*, which is very much a joint venture.

As always, thank you to my family for their pride in my work, their moral support, and their tolerance for the kind of neglect that happens when I am meeting deadlines.

And finally a big thank you to the fine yarn companies who so generously supported *Crochet Garden*. Please visit their websites for pattern ideas, newsletters, color cards, and more:

Berroco
www.berroco.com

Blue Sky Alpacas
www.blueskyalpacas.com

Brooks Farm
www.brooksfarmyarn.com

Brown Sheep Company
www.brownsheep.com

Caron International
www.naturallycaron.com

Cascade Yarns
www.cascadeyarns.com

Coats & Clark
www.coatsandclark.com

Dale of Norway
http://www.shopatron.com/home/index/1744.0.1.1

DMC
www.dmc-usa.com

Earth Arts
www.earth-arts.com

Ellen's 1/2 Pint Farm
www.ellenshalfpintfarm.com

Fiber Fanatic
fiberfanatic@hotmail.com

Ivy Brambles
www.ivybrambles.com

Judi & Co.
www.judiandco.com

Lion Brand Yarn Company
www.lionbrand.com

Louet
www.louet.com/yarns

Malabrigo
www.malabrigoyarn.com

Prism Yarns
www.prismyarn.com

Spud & Chlöe
www.spudandchloe.com

Tapetes de Lana Mill
www.tapetesdelana.com

Universal Yarn
www.universalyarn.com

Yummy Yarns
www.jellyyarns.com

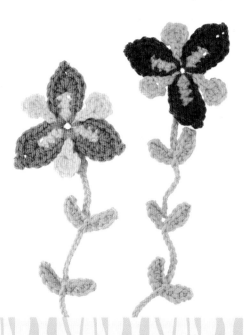

About the Author

Suzann Thompson has crocheted and knitted since childhood. In junior high, she earned a fortune (of several hundred dollars) by crocheting and selling granny square handbags. However, she later chose writing and designing over mass production. Suzann now lives with her husband and two daughters in a house filled with books and craft supplies. She teaches and writes about crochet, knitting, and polymer clay. Her first full-length crochet book, *Crochet Bouquet*, was also published by Lark Crafts. Read more about Suzann's work at www.textilefusion.com.

Index

Pick up a copy of *Crochet Bouquet* for more crochet flower fun from Suzann Thompson!

ISBN 13: 978-1-60059-124-2